UNGRATEFUL

BY

PATRICIA IFEOMA AMARAM

Editorial Midwife Publishing

Ordering Information

Quantity sales. Special discounts are available on quantity purchases by corporations, associations, and others. Contact the author at ucheuhe@yahoo.com.

Editor & Consultant

Lita P. Ward, The Editorial Midwife
LPW Editing & Consulting Services, LLC
Editorial Midwife Publishing
www.litaward.org / lpwediting@gmail.com

ISBN: 9798861893022

DEDICATION

I would like to express my sincere gratitude to God Almighty, who made my effort to be a success. I am also grateful to His Son, Jesus Christ, through whom I can do all things. Others worthy of mentioning are my parents, Engr. Pastor Patrick Amaram and Mrs. Martha Amaram, my Beloved Sons, Patrick Yidin and Paul Yidin, and well-wishers for their support and encouragement through the struggles in making this book a success.

Table of Contents

CHAPTER ONE

A Ride to Macon

Jimmy finally walked out of prison after serving 17 years of a twenty-year sentence in the Georgia State Prison of Reidsville for murder and manslaughter. Looking at the sky as a free man, he turned his head towards the prison gate. Countless times, he wondered when and if he would ever get out. Now, he asked himself if it was for real that he was out from behind that wall.

"Is this for real?" He repeated over and over again. Before he knew it, he dashed down the road as if trying to escape. A quarter mile from the prison site, he sat on a rock to catch his breath and thoughts. Relaxing his jaw on his right hand for over two hours, he thought about what it was like in the outside world. He had no idea what to do next or how he would face society. Dressed in his white baggy and raggedy white T-shirt draped over the dirty brown and white striped pants, he looked down soberly at his black sneakers missing the left strip. Clearly, he was not dressed for success, and he knew he needed help.

"Oh, Jessica, my wife, Julie, my daughter, and John, my son, will be somewhere now," he whispered. "I wish I knew where and how to find them." He wondered why Jessica had not written or visited him in prison for over ten years, even after several letters he wrote to her. Picking up his brown paper bag with his right hand, Jimmy walked across the street northbound to the closest city he could find. He waved at a couple of the automobiles driving in the direction he was heading, intending to leave the county of his imprisonment. Luckily, a Good Samaritan stopped for him as he requested a ride toward Glenville, Georgia.

"Oh!" the driver exclaimed. "Hop on in; that is my direction anyway!"

Jimmy quickly opened the passenger door and hopped into the car, noticing an infant car seat in the back. He was definitely surprised that this driver had stopped for him. A few minutes later, Jimmy felt excited riding in a car after his lengthy incarceration and being a free man. Without any conversation, he decided to generate dialogue between himself and the driver.

"My bad, I am Jimmy by name, but popularly called Jim," he said, looking in the driver's direction.

"Good to know that. My name is Elizabeth, but my friends call me Lizzy. I prefer to be addressed as Lizzy anyways," the lady smiled.

"Lizzy, what?" Jim asked.

"Lizzy McDon," she replied. "And you?"

He replied, "Jimmy Thompson, ma'am."

"Well, that's a nice name you got there!" she added.

As they journeyed through Georgia I-24 to Glenville, Jimmy asked her if that was her final destination.

"Actually, no, I am actually heading to Macon, where I reside. I only came down here to visit my grandparents, who live in Raysville, Georgia. I have not visited them for a while, so I used this Martin Luther King holiday to spend two nights with them."

"So, how was it? Did you enjoy your stay with them?" He inquired to keep the conversation going.

"Absolutely! It was fun!" She smiled.

Feeling more comfortable with Elizabeth, Jimmy asked. "Do you mind if I call you Lizzy?"

"No, I don't! In fact, I prefer Lizzy to Elizabeth, like I said earlier on." She replied.

Jimmy smiled and asked to join her in the Macon direction, of which Lizzy had no problem.

"I don't mind; having someone with me as will be great I drive. I like to have company when I drive such long distances anyway."

"How old is your son?" Jimmy asked as he turned his head to a ninety-degree angle towards her, referring to the infant sleeping in the car seat behind him.

"Little Victor, Jr. is three months old," Lizzy replied, smiling.

"Such a handsome little boy." He said, positively nodding his head.

"Well, thank you, and he is the spitting image of his father. So, do you live in Macon, or are you going for a visit?" Lizzy asked.

"Not quite," Jimmy shyly replied.

"What do you mean?" she asked.

"Uhhh," he stammered. "I -I -I mean…It's a long story, you know my story. My experiences in life are not what I want to talk about at this time."

"Spill it out, man! We are not departing from each other in the next thirty minutes, are we? We still have about two good hours to get to Macon unless you plan to get out of my car before Macon."

"No, not at all. I am going with you to Macon," Jimmy quickly replied.

"So you see, your story can not be more than two hours long. All you have to do is just be brief in your narration." She laughed.

"Okay, I got you. You don't give up, do you?   Jimmy chuckled.

"Well, I don't think it is a bad idea for us to know more about each other since we are friends now, aren't we?" Lizzy asked excitedly.

"Yeah, of course, we are now friends," Jimmy smiled.

As they continued their journey, Lizzy shared that she was from Jessup, Georgia, but lived and worked in Raysville at the medical center as a psychologist for over five years. She was recently transferred to Macon Hospital to head the behavioral health department. Shockingly, she was a widow who lost her United States Army Commission Officer husband in the Operation Free Iraq War two months before their son Victor Mcdon was born.

"Wow! It's a shame your little boy will not grow up knowing his father," Jimmy responded sorrowfully as she continued to narrate her story.

"I know it is quite unfortunate this happened to me and my little boy. I will have to answer a lot of questions from him as he grows into a teenager." She added.

"No doubt," Jimmy nodded. "He is going to want to know how he looked and how he passed away, you know?"

"Yes! And how old and tall was he when he passed away? Do I have his pictures? Where was he from? Does he have siblings, parents? And so on and so forth. I bet you it is not going to be easy." She took a deep breath and sighed.

At that point in time, baby Victor woke up crying. "Oh, my little one, you are now awake. Hold on, I know it's time to eat, and I need to take a break from driving anyways. You must be hungry by now," she added. Jimmy stretched his left hand, touching the baby's feet to calm him down. "I can see you are good with babies," she commended Jimmy.

"*How I wish I was,*" he murmured to himself silently, his thoughts flashing back to where he has been for the longest seventeen years of his life.

"We have to stop in Dublin, so I can feed the baby," said Lizzy. In a short while, they drove into Dublin; it didn't take them long to find a convenient restaurant to get refreshed.

Once seated in the restaurant, Lizzy began to breastfeed her hungry son. It took Jimmy by surprise since he was expecting her to pull out a baby bottle. Jimmy tried staring down at the floor but ended up gawking at Lizzy as she breastfed her son. It had been seventeen years since he had seen a woman or one with an exposed body part in that position or any other for that matter.

Lizzy noticed Jimmy's somewhat uncomfortable expression as she nursed her son in the restaurant. She thought he was judging her for publicly breastfeeding using only a sky-blue cover-up. "What is that look on your face?" Lizzy asked him.

"W-W-What do you mean?" he stammered.

"I mean the way you are staring at my baby and me instead of focusing on your food. I want to believe you are not one of those people who antagonize nursing mothers and speak ill about public breastfeeding." As she spoke, she tried educating Jimmy on why breastfeeding is most important for an infant and why it does not matter where and how. "What matters is the baby gets the best of it," Lizzy proudly said.

"Okay, whatever," Jimmy quickly answered as he raised both shoulders simultaneously, showing no remorse for his actions.

Lizzy grabbed her cell phone and pulled up her Facebook account. She wanted to show Jimmy that she was not alone in her efforts to breastfeed her son. "I want you to listen to this mother's story named Katie.

"Earlier today, I posted this picture of my son and I breastfeeding him uncovered in a public restaurant," Katie captioned the photo on Facebook. *"In the picture, it appears I'm staring off into the distance. In reality, I'm staring into the eyes of a woman staring back at me. She was looking at me with disgust and shaking her head*

*with judgment in an attempt to shame me and indirectly tell me without words that I was wrong and needed to cover myself. Let me clarify why I am adamant about publicly breastfeeding **MY** child. So, I am not saying everyone should breastfeed without a cover and show the world their boobs, either!"* Katie wrote.

Lizzie looked up and interjected. "If a mother is more comfortable covering herself because she feels better doing so, then I totally support her in that as well." She continued with Katie's post.

"With that being said, I post these types of pictures for the mother that tried breastfeeding uncovered once, yet was shamed, stared and pointed at, heard nasty comments, and was asked to leave or cover herself up."

"In my opinion, Katie is right; it is a woman's right to breastfeed, which is also the baby's right to eat," Lizzy commented, pausing to ensure Jimmy was still listening and following the story.

Jimmy tried his best, pretending he was okay with it, looking interested and engaged. However, he just wanted Lizzy to finish the story so they could leave. He was more tired now and still concerned about his next move.

Lizzy continued reading Katie's post. *"No person should be isolated and shunned because they're eating. Is it not certainly easier to avert your eyes from a displeasing sight rather than suggest or demand a mother and child remove themselves from your presence? How pompous and selfish is that? Just look away!"* Katie wrote.

Katie also explained why she believed children needed to experience breastfeeding. *"People need to understand that breast milk and breastfeeding is and should forever be the first and best choice for both mom and baby."*

"So, you see, Jimmy, it is not just about the mom doing it for a show or attention. It is what's best for my son and I."

After his education about breastfeeding, Jimmy realized Lizzy was doing the right thing for her baby, not minding where it was.

"I also have another story to tell you if you are willing to listen," Lizzy said.

"Uh, okay. Um, sure. I am enjoying your stories," Jimmy replied. "You can go ahead." After that first reprimand from her, Jimmy did not dare to make her mad again. He was exhausted but could not bite the hand that was feeding him.

Lizzy started her storyline. "In a dense forest lived a fierce lion. He was ruthless. One day, the lion was caught in a hunter's trap. One by one, many animals passed by. "Please help me!" pleaded the lion. But none of the animals listened to his cries. After a while, a man happened to enter the forest and saw the lion.

The lion said, "I will die of hunger and suffocation. Please help me out, oh kind man!"

The man thought about it for a moment.

"I assure you I will never harm you. Please help me now. The hunter will be anytime now," said the lion.

The man felt sorry for the lion and set the beast free. As soon as the lion was free, he let out a fierce roar. "I have been trapped in the cage for a long time. I am hungry and will have to eat you," said the lion, looking at the man.

"But you promised that you would not harm me," said the man in a meek tone.

"Yes, I said that. But only to convince you to free me. Now, I am terribly hungry," said the lion.

The terrified man thought quickly. He said, "Alright, you can eat me. But let a judge decide if you are right to eat the person who rescued you."

The lion agreed because he was sure that no animal would speak against him. Just then, a jackal came that way, and the lion asked the jackal to be the judge. He agreed and addressed the lion.

"Sir, would you please show me how it all happened?"

The lion was only too willing and entered the cage and closed the cage door. The jackal immediately bolted the cage from the outside.

"Now the lion is trapped again. Run away, you foolish man! And never offer help to anyone without thinking," said the jackal. The frightened man ran for his life. And the ungrateful lion was trapped in the cage again. The hunter came and took the lion away to his circus. The lesson from this story is that ingratitude is an integral part of society. If you ask most people if they are ungrateful, they will probably reply, "Of course not!" However, this attitude is so ingrained in their lives they cannot openly admit it or even realize that they are ungrateful. Probably for the sake of self-defense. But how can you tell if *you* are ungrateful? Are there things that identify ingratitude? And if so, what can you do about it?"

Lizzy continued explaining the matter as she quoted Webster's definition of *Ingratitude* as: "Forgetfulness of, or poor return for, kindness received. It can also be defined as not appreciating or valuing what you have been given or possess. *Unexpressed* gratitude is also ingratitude! In today's fast-paced world, most people do not have time for thankfulness. Their main priorities are work, traffic, family, soccer practice, doctor appointments, and countless others. They seem to have no time to thank others."

Before we continue with our story, consider the following:

1. Have you ever given someone a gift and not received thanks for it?

2. Have you ever been in a grocery store or restaurant without being thanked for your business?

3. Have you ever felt unappreciated by family or friends or at your workplace? If so, how did it make you feel? Probably not very good, right?

4. How often do we get up in the morning with a big smile, thanking God for whatever He has blessed us with?

5. How often have you sat in your living room with your family watching some TV shows, having harmless, funny fights with your siblings, but do not thank God for blessing you with another evening with your family?

6. How often did your mom cook something you disliked the most, but you sat down with her and really enjoyed it ONLY because your mom cooked it for you and you complimented her?

7. How many times you've thanked the Almighty Father for blessing you with a childhood full of sweet memories?

8. How many times have you really wanted to complain, but your mouth was shut tight because you just lost count of all the blessings?

"Can you really thank Him enough?" Lizzy asked Jimmy, who could not utter a word. "Well, it is time to get back onto the road because I don't like driving late at night anyways," Lizzy said.

As they continued the drive, Lizzy continued the discussion without delay. "We can spend hours and hours complaining how miserable our life is, how unfair our faith had been with us, and how we really don't deserve this kind of life." Don't you think so?" She asked Jimmy.

"Well, life is such…" Jimmy tried to reply. But Lizzy jumped back onto her soapbox and continued her ideals of ungratefulness.

"We complain about so many things in life, such as losing a job or not getting the job we always wanted, not having a luxurious life, or getting into a fight with a best friend. Complain, complain, and complain about not getting the love of our life we desire, not having friends who stick with us through thin and thick. Oh, I am more! We complain about not getting the grades we aimed for, not having understanding parents, not having enough money, and being unable to afford something we want. All we do is complain, not showing gratitude, but can we spend the same amount of time determining everything with all sincerity, subtracting all the mishaps, and adding all the blessings? Trust me on one thing; after all the additions and subtractions, the blessings and fortunate things we own still outnumber the mishaps we encounter."

As Lizzy continued her analysis and dissertation on being ungrateful, Jimmy thought about his family and what he would do next. No home, job, or family. His future did not look promising. So what should he be grateful for? As she talked, he peered out the window, and his mind wandered back to where his family could be. He wondered if his kids would even remember what he looked like.

"Now, Jimmy, imagine a family of four daughters and two sons. You enter their house and see a nicely decorated warm house, well organized with expensive furnishings. All four daughters, aged

15, 12, 9, and 7, sit in the family room, engaged with the television or computer gadgets. The three and four-year-old baby brothers are taking their nap while their mom, with a smile, gives the final touches to their dinner preparation. Dad just came home from work and is ungratefully leaning against the kitchen counter, telling his wife everything about his day at work. Just because his day at work was hectic. Then suddenly gets mad at his wife for having six children, which makes him work his ass off! He forgets some couples cannot even afford to produce one child! I am just saying that we should be more grateful because matters could always be worse."

Finally, Lizzy and Jimmy made it to their destination of Macon with all the food for thought provided along the way. Lizzy turned to Jimmy and asked him where he could be dropped off, but she got no response. A minute after, Lizzy said, "You still haven't answered my question." She wondered if all was alright with him because his countenance changed, now looking very depressed. "Is everything alright?" Lizzy asked.

"You can drop me off anywhere," Jimmy replied, picking up his brown paper bag from between his legs and holding it underneath.

The bag suddenly ripped, and his belongings fell into the car's floorboard.

"What do you mean by anywhere?"

"It's a long story," Jimmy mumbled as he tried gathering his clothes.

Not wanting to push Jimmy, Lizzy said, "Okay, what's going to happen is I can put you into a motel tonight because it's very late now, and I got to get some rest before resuming my job tomorrow morning. I will come to check on you during my break hours tomorrow. You can order anything you want from room service, and I will pay when I come tomorrow."

"Um, wow, thanks. I appreciate this because I had no other option," Jimmy sadly admitted.

Lizzy drove to the motel close to her subdivision, where she paid for a room to keep Jimmy safe and comfortable for the night before driving into her subdivision to get some rest after their long ride.

Jimmy thought to himself. *Finally, some good luck is coming my way. This could be the start of a new life.*

CHAPTER TWO

Jimmy in Macon

Taking off his white, raggedy-looking T-shirt to have a nice hot shower, Jimmy heard a knock on the door. "Yo' who is that?!" Jimmy yelled. But, the knock came again. "Hold on, I'm comin'," he said as he snatched open the door. Lo and behold, it was Tammy, a female employee from the motel. *Oh, what a nice, good-looking creature,* Jimmy thought, being that he had been incarcerated for such a long time and had no opportunity to behold such a sigh for quite a while. Tammy walked into the room with a tray of food and drinks that Jimmy had ordered when he arrived at his room.

"I brought your order, sir," Tammy smiled.

"Oh, okay! You can drop it on the table," Jimmy smiled back, pointing directly to the table beneath the TV hanging on the wall.

"Alrighty, sir," Tammy replied as she placed the tray. She noticed that Jimmy was staring at her just a little too hard. It made her feel slightly uncomfortable, which was her cue to exit. "Enjoy!" she said as she ditched out of the room.

Jimmy looked at the food and ravenously tore into it as if it was his last meal on Earth. He completely forgot about the beautiful young lady who had just captivated his attention. He could not remember the last time he had any of his favorites, fried chicken, black-eyed peas, mashed potatoes, and honey-buttered cornbread. Then to top it all off, Georgia's finest peach cobbler and iced tea. Jimmy knew he would sleep like a baby with a warm cozy bed and a full stomach.

Lizzy made it to the hotel during her break hour the next day, as promised. After a warm greeting, she jumped directly into the question, eager to know why Jimmy was homeless. Jimmy told her he had been incarcerated and was lucky to be the fiftieth of the inmates released when the president celebrated his late mother's one-year remembrance day.

He waited for her to lecture and kick him out of the motel room she had paid for. Surprisingly, Lizzy was not taken aback by Jmmy's prison record, which shocked him. "Well, I would not want you to take a leisurely stroll in a big city like this, or any metropolitan city for that matter. You will find it difficult to survive as a homeless person living on the street. Besides, you will get yourself entangled with nothing less than trouble. With that being said, you can stay with me until you find a safe place to live." Lizzy stated. She was a caring, benevolent, kind, and generous woman, so she believed her offer was the right thing to do.

"Huh?! Wait! What?! Can this be for real?" Jimmy murmured to himself, wiping his eyes before the tears came. He was excited and bewildered about the offer because he could not believe he would have a roof over his head that fast and with a complete stranger. *"But how?! This is a gold mine I received on a gold platter. Whoa! Just like that?"* He thought to himself.

Lizzy took some steps towards the window, looking out of it to give him some time to think about her offer. However, she needed an answer as soon as possible, knowing time was not on her side to drive back to her job. "Well, you can think about it if you are unsure if to accept my offer. I just have to get back to my office now," She replied and shrugged.

"Oh no! I accept your offer. Yes, ma'am! Let me grab my stuff!" Jimmy shouted as he rushed into the closet and grabbed his brown paper bag. Quickly, he put on his shoes and headed towards the door to exit. It was definitely summer in Georgia, and the hot sticky air stuck to their clothes as they dashed to the car. Lizzy drove to her home, showed Jimmy around, and introduced him to her pet, Smarts, a full-blooded German Sheppard. Then, she excused herself before returning to work because her lunch break had been over for a while.

Jimmy could not believe how things had worked out for him. He looked around the beautiful two-story home offered to him temporarily. To this day, Jimmy could not remember anything good happening to him in the past years. The bedroom Lizzy gave him was comfortably furnished with a television and mini refrigerator filled with snacks and drinks. She had offered him her entire home without question. However, somehow, he still questioned her intentions. It must have been his past, still holding onto him. Jimmy had not trusted anyone in over two decades and wasn't quite ready to start now. Deciding to take a short walk around the subdivision while Lizzy was at work, he noticed the well-kept lawns with blooming flowers. It had been a long time since Jimmy could walk outside alone and enjoy pleasant scenery. Within a short time, he returned to the house, spending the rest of the day watching television shows.

It was dark. The automatic spotlights had come on, giving the living room a beautiful, lightly dimmed scene. Jimmy relaxed, watching the television, when he noticed Lizzy's car lights cruising up the driveway. He jumped up from the couch, walked to the door, and opened it as he ushered her in with a huge smile.

"Oh, thank you for getting the door. Whew! I am beat! You're still awake?" Lizzy asked.

"Oh yes! I just didn't feel like going to bed yet," He answered. "I was kind of waiting up to see those big brown eyes of little Victor. He's not with you? Jimmy inquired.

"No, not tonight. My son is with my friend, who babysits for me here in this subdivision. I will introduce her to you in the morning."

"Okay, then," Jimmy replied.

"So, how did your day go today?" Lizzy asked, wondering if he had made any plans.

"It was great. I took a walk around here and watched TV. Just relaxed a bit today. You know?"

"Good to know! Well, I will have to excuse myself so I can shower and get some rest. I have another busy day tomorrow." She explained.

"Oh, I understand! But before you go, can you spare me some cash? I need to walk to the store to pick up some more drinks."

"Unfortunately, I don't have any cash on me. I am used to paying with my debit or credit cards. Hmmm, I can't remember the last time I used cash," Lizzy chuckled. "Besides, it is too late now; all the stores near the subdivision are closed already."

Jimmy sobered up instantly, shaking his head, now agitated. He murmured under his breath as Lizzy walked away towards her bedroom. Lizzy thought to herself; *before I left this morning, the house was fully stocked with drinks and food. I sure hope this does not become a habit of his.*

The next day Lizzy and Jimmy drove to Dr. Susan's home, where Lizzy introduced Jimmy to Dr. Susan as her best friend and nanny. Lizzy could hear her son happily cooing in his crib as soon as they walked in. Laying in the solid wood baby crib, baby Victor finally laid eyes on his mother, and his eyes brightened up as soon as he saw her. Being who she is and having the same caring, benevolent, and kind character as her friend Lizzy, Dr. Susan welcomed Jimmy warmly.

Jimmy looked around Dr. Susan's home and was amazed that her home was even more beautiful than Lizzy's. Almost every part of the living and family rooms was covered in immaculate wall art. He thought he was in an art gallery instead of a home. He kindly complimented Dr. Susan on how beautiful and elegant her home was. He even inquired if there was any historical information about the house. At the same time, Lizzy continued tending to her son.

"Dr. Susan, you have a magnificent home here," Jimmy stated.

"Thanks, Jimmy," she smiled.

"Oh! I forgot to tell you that Dr. Susan prefers to be called Susan, so don't sound all official," Lizzy giggled.

"Noted; I will try to keep it as simple as possible," Jimmy laughed.

"What can I offer you, Jimmy, this morning?" Susan asked.

Jimmy requested a cup of coffee as he sat in one of the comfortable living room chairs. A couple of minutes later, Susan presented coffee and a sandwich to him, which Jimmy pounced on without wasting time. He didn't show any gratitude towards anything given to him by Susan, which was surprising since he started out being polite. Not even a word of thanks nor a bright facial expression was noticed because, somehow, Jimmy believed it was his by his right to receive it. Susan noticed this unpleasant and rude attitude from Jimmy and wondered why he acted that way.

"Jimmy, are you alright?" Susan asked.

"Yeah, why do you ask? What do you mean?" Jimmy replied in a bizarre demeanor as he scoffed down the breakfast.

Susan continued talking to him, trying to discover the issue with him. She told Jimmy that we live in a world where everyone is in search of happiness, and each individual has their own approach this journey takes. For some, the search begins with their life experience, books, and privileges. For others, it comes through service. She explained why the most common way of seeking gratification is by accumulating "treasures and valuables." Materialism, though, is bought at a cost.

Lizzy had finally finished feeding and tending to little Victor's needs. Before gently placing him back in his crib, she tenderly gave sleeping Victor one more snuggle. She picked up her purse to dash to her teaching job and walked towards Susan and Jimmy; she asked Jimmy if he was ready to return to the house.

"Oh, he doesn't have to leave now. Actually, he can walk back to your house later. We are having an enlightening discussion. Right, Jimmy? Besides, if he goes home, he might be lonely." Susan smiled.

Surprisingly, Jimmy actually bought the idea to hang out with Susan for a while.

"Okay, then see you all later," Lizzy said as she hurriedly dashed out the door.

At this point, Jimmy was done with the breakfast he was offered, and Susan cleared the table in a hurry to get back to her conversation with Jimmy. She inhaled and grinned as she took her seat across from Jimmy. She studied him a little longer, as if she wanted to say more, but didn't know where to start since he was not adding to their conversation.

"Do you have something to say?" Susan asked.

He shook his head, "Nope," rubbing both his palms on his head and face as he took a more relaxed posture on the couch.

She wanted to say more to see if she could break his silence as she turned and sighed again. She looked through the large glass window as an elderly couple strolled by on their morning walk.

"Would you like anything else, or are you okay with the coffee for now?" She asked.

"What else do you have?" he asked, not even looking away from the television.

"Well, I have some rice and fried chicken that I don't have to cook. It is already prepared, and I have it in my refrigerator."

As a sign of accepting her offer, Jimmy shrugged his shoulders. Once again, his ingratitude was on full display, which Susan noticed immediately for the second time. But that did not stop her from dashing into her kitchen to present him with a plate of homecooked food. And unfortunately, again, not a word of gratitude.

The morning light cast a harsh glare on the scarred glass table and the polished hardwood living room floor. Susan returned her attention to Jimmy. "You agreed you would spend time with me today instead of going home. Isn't that correct?" Susan asked.

"Well, yeah, duh," he replied sarcastically.

Susam was shocked when instead of showing gratitude for favors given to him, it was the opposite, as if she owed him. *Is it that he is always like this? Or he has a personality disorder?* Susan wondered.

Suddenly there was a knock coming from the entrance door.

"Hold on," Susan replied as she walked towards the door. "Who is it?" she asked.

The female voice responded, "It's Mimi!"

"Oh, come in, come in!" Susan shouted.

Mimi picking up her traveling bag dashed in through the double swinging entrance doors into the living room. Susan introduced her niece to Jimmy and explained that she had come to spend time with her every summer. He nodded his head without uttering a word; as Mimi found her way to her favorite room in the house.

Tension darkened Susan's expression as she rubbed the back of her neck with her silky soft hand. *What is the matter with this man?* Her mind wondered. She was still trying to figure it out. Susan sat back, straightened her shoulders, and forced a smile at Jimmy. At this point, Susan had reasons to continue her gratitude conversation with Jimmy, explaining how a society that feels entitled to what it receives does not satisfactorily describe gratitude. She stated, "The lack of gratitude is contagious and passed from generation to generation."

Conversely, she made him understand that gratitude is also viral and has been found to significantly and favorably sway and influence not just relationships but one's own emotional status. Gratitude has its own charismatic desire and appeal. However, if we fail to choose or abandon it, we choose ingratitude by default. It's just a pity that millions make this choice every day.

These scenarios of Jimmy's ungrateful actions reminded Susan of her experiences with Uncle Laz and his wife, Janet. It was funny how her uncle and aunt started treating her differently after marriage. They both felt she was married to a wealthy man. They would randomly request one thing or the other without asking her if she even had the funds to address their financial issues. Even after she went out of her way to assist them financially, Uncle Laz and Janet never showed any sign of gratitude. Instead, they asked for more and more. She would cook her cousins' favorite dishes and bring them to her uncle's house for everyone. Her cousins were usually not allowed to visit her but only on special occasions, like Easter, Christmas, and

Memorial Day celebrations. And when they did visit her, they would have the time of their lives with many gifts to take home with them.

Her uncle made life so unbearable for her. However, Susan had no choice but to live with it, because that was the only family she had after her parents and only brother died in a car crash. Life took a different turn for her at that point; she started filling up her cousins' lives with as much love, care, and happiness as much as she could offer. Even when Uncle Laz lost his job, Susan endeavored to handle his bill without complaint. Still, Uncle Laz did not once show gratitude to Susan. No matter how Susan tried to assist her uncle, it was still imperfect in Uncle Laz's and his wife's eyes. Susan remembered her frequent arguments with her husband because of her Uncle's behavior and her frustration at her uncle and aunt, who would keep interfering in her life.

Susan recalled when she was just 15 years old and growing up fast. The time came when she felt the need for someone to care for her and take her through life as a teenager since she was an orphan. Susan needed someone to answer all the questions a teenager and young woman had about life. Unfortunately, she had to figure out life independently because her Uncle's wife, Jane, never cared for her. So many things can't be explained in black and white, so many painful memories from teenage to adulthood. When even Susan's fundamental necessities were not cared for, she came to a point where she embraced summer jobs as a teenager to provide her basic necessities. Susan's heart just about jumped out of her chest when the sudden flashback of the domestic violence by her uncle at her teenage stage was never addressed till she grew into adulthood and got married.

Her thoughts were interrupted by snoring sounds from Jimmy as he laid his head back, getting himself more relaxed on the sofa. Quiet vibrations, whistling, grumbling, snorting, and rumbling were all just affecting Jimmy, who was trying all he could to nap.

"Jimmy! Hello, Jimmy! Jimmy?!" Susan called out, but Jimmy was now fast asleep. She decided to go about her daily chores and care for little Victor, who woke up not too long later. Susan pondered repeatedly, wondering the kind of personality Jimmy had. Even though she didn't know his history or background, and it was their first time meeting, it still made her a little crazy. She could not grasp his state of mind as she stood and stared at the sleeping and snoring Jimmy. "But why is his behavior this odd?" She mumbled as she walked away to check on her niece.

Lizzy called Susan from her office two hours later to check on her son and Jimmy. Susan gave a good report of the baby but told Lizzy how concerned she was with Jimmy's attitude. Jimmy had left the house after finishing his morning and noon nap. Susan was glad he was gone since she had become perturbed by his behavior. She asked Lizzy a couple of questions that Lizzy had no answers to because she had just met Jimmy a day before.

"I am still trying to study him," Lizzy responded. She explained to Susan how she met Jimmy and her little history about him. Susan became nervous and anxious, realizing she had been with such a fellow alone in her home. While listening to Lizzy, Susan began to panic, with rapid breathing and near hyperventilation. Her stomach felt like it was full of knots.

"Oh, my God," she murmured, shaking her head. As Lizzy continued the discussion, Susan's panic attack worsened as she motioned for Lizzy to stop talking. Lizzy could hear that Susan was upset and tried to calm her and apologize.

"No, no, no! This is a huge problem," Susan gasped. "I need to calm down. I really don't feel so good," she moaned and retreated to the kitchen. "I will talk to you more about it when you come to pick up the baby."

Susan tried practicing mindfulness techniques she had learned from psychologist Amy Sullivan in an online Zoom conference session. Mindfulness teaches you how to stay in the present instead of fear and uncertainty of the present and future. Sullivan said it was an excellent method for handling anxiety and nervousness.

Plopping down at her breakfast nook, Susan pondered the next steps regarding the information she just gathered about Jimmy. For a minute, she didn't think she could let it go and would need time to think more about this serious matter.

"Knock! Knock! Knock!"

Looking exhausted, Lizzy knocked on Susan's front door. She was still worried about Susan and her thoughts about how she allowed an ex-con to reside in her home. So, Lizzy prepared herself for a lecture or tongue-lashing from her protective friend.

Trying to relieve the tension, Susan chose to put their friendship first."Oh, my dear friend, Lizzy. You must be hungry now. Can I make you some soup?" Susan asked.

"No, my dear friend. But thank you so much. I already had my dinner. I'm just tired and need some rest," Lizzy responded.

"Well, the good news is you can get some rest. After all, tomorrow is a federal holiday," Susan said.

"Yes, Lord!" Lizzy smiled.

Personally, Susan was eager to discuss Jimmy with her friend, but seeing how exhausted she was decided to let her be. Lizzy looked at her watch; it was just half past eight. She looked forward to getting home and being able to rest the next day. The two friends moved to the living room, where baby Victor was in his crib. As Lizzy reached down to pick up baby Victor, she asked Susan when Jimmy left the house. Susan stated he left around four that evening. Lizzy wondered where he had ventured and hoped he didn't meet trouble and mischief when he arrived at his destination. She was too tired to think or talk about Jimmy, so she set her eyes toward the door and waited for the next wave of energy to carry her. Finally, Lizzy picked up her purse and baby Victor, bidding Susan goodbye. She especially thanked her for not lecturing her about Jimmy.

CHAPTER THREE

Finally Fed Up

Lizzy spent the whole night staring at the ceiling before drifting off to sleep a few hours near daybreak. Now listening to the whistles from the birds outside her bedroom window, she tried adjusting her eyes to the bright Georgia sun. The weather was as perfect as it could get this time of year in Georgia. The gentle breeze from the cool morning air made her so relaxed.

"Knock! Knock!"

Jimmy was at her bedroom door, needing a shaving stick for his overgrown beard. He made the request without the courtesy of saying good morning.

"Good morning, Jimmy! How was your night?" Lizzy asked through the door.

"Uh, yeah, good morning." He replied.

"I'll see what I can find. Let me slip something on, and I will check my bathroom." Lizzy momentarily wondered what a weird character Jimmy was and felt concerned. Once she found one of her disposable razors, she handed it to Jimmy. Lizzy went back to bed, wriggling under the sheets, and got comfortable enough for more rest. Baby Victor was still sleeping, so she needed to take advantage of it. Pondering over Jimmy's actions, she meditated on how Jimmy's ungratefulness could ruin him the more.

It could fuel dissatisfaction and negatively impact his relationships. The act of ingratitude will take a toll on anyone's destiny. Lizzy felt Jimmy needed to better understand the impacts of being ungrateful, the disadvantages of being ungrateful, the importance of practicing gratitude, and how mindfulness could help.

As the thoughts sank into her, she became restless and could not go back to sleep. She took some deep breaths and stretched, elongating her body for a few seconds with her eyes closed. She bent her knees, placed her feet flat on the bed, rolled onto her side, used both hands, pushed herself up to a sitting position, and took a deep breath one more time. Swinging both legs onto the floor, she pressed her feet into the plush carpet and, again, mindfully, took another deep breath. Calmly, she strolled into her restroom for a refreshing shower.

Staring at the mirror, she brushed her teeth. Lizzy still could not get her thoughts of Jimmy's character out of her head. She pondered how to educate him on how to show gratitude, being thankful or appreciative. It was vital for him to know it is also a quality we can cultivate, making an attitude of gratitude a trait we can develop.

"Hmm! I surely hope he listens and understands what I have to say to him," she murmured, drying her hands on the white towel hanging on the restroom rail. Lizzy dashed into the kitchen as she took some time to prepare breakfast for herself and Jimmy, who was freshening up on his side of the house.

"Jimmy! Jimmy! Breakfast is ready!" Lizzy shouted.

Not long after, Jimmy joined her in the dining room, and they started the day with a befitting meal.

"Do you have plans for today?" Lizzy inquired.

"Not really. Why do you ask?"

"Oh! Just asking," she replied. She explained that she might hang out by the pool in the subdivision later in the day and invited him to join her if he so wished.

"Well, that's not a bad idea," he casually replied, barely looking up front his plate. He seemed very uninterested.

"There you go again," Lizzy murmured, noticing the level of ingratitude in Jimmy's voice and persona. "Can you not just say thank you, I appreciate it, or even give a compliment? Why is it like that with you?" She asked in disappointment. But Jimmy remained mute without remorse. She explained to him that we are all guilty of letting the stresses of daily life get in the way of understanding, comprehending, and expressing gratitude. Naturally, we often forget to stop and think about the things we are most grateful for.

Lizzy shared with him the importance of a morning gratitude ritual that allowed him to start the day grounded in gratitude, appreciating the small things people did for him and even appreciating the good and the bad experiences in life because it was all for a reason.

"Listen, Jimmy. The journey to gratefulness may not happen overnight, but you need to start working on it for your own good," she advised. "Besides, now that you are a free man, what are your plans?" Lizzy asked.

"I don't understand what you mean by plans," Jimmy replied.

"What you plan to do for a living, like a job, sir?"

"Um, I am still not looking because I don't have any credentials to apply for a job. Neither did I acquire any before being arrested." He explained.

"Are you saying you don't have a family member you can go to retrieve your credentials, like your diploma or certificate?" She asked.

"I mean, I no longer have access to any. While in prison, I received a letter from my younger sister Julie stating that the family house where our documents and pictures were kept was burnt to ashes accidentally," he explained.

On hearing this, Lizzy dropped the subject and became more sympathetic. She was at a loss for words to address the situation. Lizzy pondered more and more on how to help Jimmy out of his situation. However, despite his helpless situation, the more she thought about him and tried to help, he still displayed his ungratefulness. This only frustrated Lizzy more. Then Lizzy thought networking among her colleagues and friends would aid him in getting a job and on his feet. Within a few weeks, Lizzy acquired Jimmy a job near the subdivision, and it would only take him five minutes to walk to his job.

"Lizzy! Where are you, Lizzy?" Jimmy yelled from the living room. He was not satisfied with the nature of the job Lizzy got for him after hearing from the human resources department that he would be a janitor in the county hospital.

As soon as Lizzy reached the living room, Jimmy started his rant. "Why would you get me a janitor's job? That's embarrassing!" Why not a bigger-paying job? Huh? Why??"

"Jimmy, it wasn't easy to get this job for you. Remember, you have no credentials. You were offered this opportunity because of my good relationship with the county general hospital's director. He only gave you this job because of me!" She tried to explain.

"Nope! I won't do this!" He exclaimed.

"Just take this job at the moment to keep yourself going. I will keep my ears open for better jobs."

Lizzy calmly tried to convince and console Jimmy for the next hour, but he was not giving in to that idea. He insisted that Lizzy get him a better opportunity than being a janitor. Lizzy was so disappointed at his approach and response to the gratitude shown to him. She educated him on how he should always be grateful. She said, "Being alive today is enough to be thankful!" She explained how the tips will help focus his attention on setting his personal gratitude challenge.

"But why bother with gratitude?" Jimmy asked.

"To answer this question, it is important to first know the benefits of gratitude, ingratitude, or being ungrateful. Lizzy added that there are many ways in which being ungrateful obstructs us. Besides fueling dissatisfaction or discontent to negatively impact our relationships, ingratitude takes a toll. "You definitely need to understand the impacts of being ungrateful, the importance of practicing gratitude, and how mindfulness can help you develop your mindset," she added.

Without skipping a beat, Jimmy nonchalantly turned to Lizzy, openly showing his disinterest, and asked, "Can you loan me some money? Honestly, I will pay you back," Jimmy said.

Bewildered at his boldness and gall, Lizzy shot back. "How do you intend to pay me back? I mean, you are already stating that you will not take the job I helped you obtain. So, please explain this."

"Well, when I get a job, I will pay you back then!" He said in a hateful tone.

"So when and where are you getting the job, sir?"

"I ain't applied anywhere yet, but I know I will find one soon!"

Lizzy reminded Jimmy of not having credentials to support his application and current societal status. Since he was an ex-con, acquiring one by himself would not be easy. Suddenly, Jimmy became more furious. He continued acting as if he was entitled to the money and should be given whatever he requested. Seeing his actions, Lizzy was somewhat fearful of what may happen if she did not comply. So, once again, she gave in to his behavior and gave him what cash she had on hand.

Moments passed, and you could cut the thick tension in the room with a butter knife. Lizzy stood up from her seat, hoping he wouldn't say anything. Then she saw the smug look on his face and knew he had a long way to go when it came to being grateful.

"I need to do some paperwork, so can you walk Smart around the neighborhood for me, please?" Lizzy requested politely.

"Yeah, sure!" Jimmy answered.

"Could you also stop by Susan's house to pick up Victor's medications? I left them on the dining room table last night. I already called her, and she said you can stop by for them. I appreciate you doing this for me," she added, hoping he would pick up on her act of gratitude.

"That's okay! I shall be on my way now," he replied, accepting with all pleasure. He dashed out of the house through the backyard exit, knowing it was another opportunity to hang out with Susan. He didn't care for her long conversations, but she sure could cook. Jimmy hurriedly took Smart, walked him through the neighborhood, and stopped by Susan's house.

"Knock! Knock! Who is home?" He asked.

"Hold on a minute!" Susan responded. As she opened her entrance door, Jimmy stood holding Smart's leash. "Good morning

Jimmy! Hi Smart!" Susan greeted them, bending and rubbing the pet's head. Smart wagged his tail in excitement, whining, pulling on the leash as he was excited to see Susan.

"Come on in," Susan said as she led the pair into the family room. "Have a seat and make yourself comfortable," she requested. She entertained him with a cup of coffee and a muffin, as requested by Jimmy when he was asked by Susan if she could get him anything.

"So, how is my friend Lizzy?" Susan smiled.

"She is okay; she needs to take care of Victor before we hang out by the pool."

"Okay, I will call her later in the day. Thanks for letting me know that."

"Well, me and Smart will head on out now," Jimmy replied as he walked towards the door holding Smart by his leash. No "thanks for the coffee" or "I appreciate your hospitality" passed through Jimmy's mind or lips.

Susan shook her head as she watched Jimmy and Smart stroll down the street, both without a care in the world. She could only hope he would get his act together sooner than later.

Jimmy admired the beautiful homes with landscaped yards as he walked through the neighborhood. He imagined hitting the lottery and moving his family into one of the homes, buying expensive cars, and having more money than he could count. So caught up in his daydream and not realizing he was already back at Lizzy's house, Jimmy was startled when he heard her voice from the front yard.

"Hi, Jimmy! How did it go? Were you able to pick up Victor's medication?" Lizzy asked.

"Oh, yeah! Here it is," he replied as he reached into his pants pocket and handed the medication to Lizzy. She collected the medication and attended to Victor. Afterward, they all prepared and headed out for the afternoon gathering at the pool.

Walking back home from the afternoon festivities was as quiet as a funeral processional. Lizzy observed Jimmy, who had nothing to say. "Did you enjoy our time and company at the pool and restaurant?" Lizzy inquired. She reached into Victor's stroller and pulled his blanket back over his legs as he tried to kick it off again. There was a cool breeze, and she did not want him to have a rough night from his asthma.

"Uh, yeah," he replied.

"Which part did you like the best?

"Hmm. I don't know. I guess all of it." Jimmy replied reluctantly.

Lizzy noticed his temperament would not improve, so she handed him some notes, as seen in the following three chapters. She had compiled the information from a psychology seminar she had attended two months earlier. Lizzy advised him to go through the note and offered him the opportunity to attend the seminar if he wished.

"Do I really need to read this?" Jimmy scoffed.

"Yes, Jimmy! I believe you need this! It just doesn't seem as if you are getting it, Jimmy. My friend Susan and I have given you golden opportunities to get on your feet and start a new life. But, somehow, you just cannot see it. Nor can you see how your ungratefulness could land you right back where I picked you up from."

Shocked at how Lizzy finally stood up to him, Jimmy opened the notes and began reading. This was the first time he had seen Lizzy like this, and he knew she meant business.

CHAPTER FOUR

Clarity on Ungratefulness

Defining *Ungratefulness:* Ungratefulness or ingratitude refers to the lack of appreciation or acknowledgment of the benefits, favors, or kindness shown to someone. It is a negative trait that can cause harm to relationships and lead to a sense of entitlement. Ungratefulness can manifest in various forms, such as taking things for granted, failing to say thank you, or disregarding others' efforts.

The Root of Ungratefulness: Ungratefulness is a sophisticated emotional state that is often connected to a variety of factors, such as poor self-esteem, enviousness, or a sense of entitlement. It can manifest in many ways, including a lack of appreciation for one's blessings and a tendency to take others for granted. At its core, ungratefulness is a negative state of mind that can have long-lasting effects on our personal, social, and professional relationships.

One of the primary causes of ungratefulness is a one-sided perception of reality. People who struggle with ungratefulness often have unrealistic expectations of themselves and others. They may have a distorted view of what is "normal" or "fair" in terms of their personal relationships or professional achievements. For example, they may believe they are entitled to success and that any setbacks or failures are due to external factors beyond their control. These unrealistic expectations can create a sense of dissatisfaction and a lack of appreciation for what one has.

Another factor that contributes to ungratefulness is a lack of self-awareness. People who are not self-aware may not understand their own emotions and behaviors, which can lead to a lack of appreciation or gratitude for others. Additionally, people who lack self-awareness may be more likely to view themselves as victims of their circumstances rather than taking responsibility for their choices and actions. This can create a sense of entitlement, which can further exacerbate feelings.

The Causes of Ungratefulness

Several factors may make one display ingratitude; some factors could be attributed to one's upbringing, and some could be due to innate traits one is born with. Some significant causes of ungratefulness are highlighted below.

1. *Self-Centeredness:* When we're too focused on ourselves, our problems, and our needs, it can be challenging to recognize the blessings and good things in our lives. As such, self-centeredness may lead to ungratefulness.

2. *Lack of Mindfulness:* Being mindful means being fully present and aware of what's happening around us. When we're not mindful, we can miss out on the good things in life, such as the beauty of nature, the love of our family and friends, and the small acts of kindness from others.

3. *Unrealistic Expectations:* Sometimes, we expect so much from ourselves and others that we fail to appreciate what we have. When we're always looking for more, we may never feel

satisfied or grateful for what we already have. And this finally nurtures the feeling of ingratitude.

4. *Focusing on the Negative:* If we only look at the negatives in our lives, we will have difficulty feeling grateful for what we still have. For instance, ungrateful people tend to be so tough on themselves that they hardly acknowledge what people around them or even themselves have achieved over time to the extent that they only focus on the bit negative part.

5. *Growing up in a Culture of Ungratefulness*: Some cultures tend to be more prone to ungratefulness than others, and growing up in such a culture can make it challenging to learn how to cultivate gratefulness.

6. *Expecting Things to Come Easily*: We may take for granted the things we didn't have to work hard to achieve or acquire.

7. *Believing in Entitlement*: When we believe that we're entitled to certain things or that the world owes us something, it becomes much harder to feel grateful. For instance, people who are always entitled to services and actions will hardly appreciate help from those around them.

8. *Lack of Understanding of What Gratitude Means*: Without a clear understanding of what gratitude is and why it's essential, it can be tough to cultivate the habit of feeling grateful.

9. *Comparing Ourselves to Others*: When we focus too much on what others have, we may feel jealous or resentful instead of grateful for what we have.

10. *Experiencing Trauma or Hardship*: It can be tough to feel grateful when we're going through a difficult time or have experienced significant trauma.

11. *Depression and Mental Health Conditions*: Some mental health conditions can make it hard to feel emotions such as gratitude, happiness, and joy. Mental conditions such as post stress-trauma disorders (PSTDs) and schizophrenic complications make one detached from the norm of human feelings and emotions.

12. *Busyness and Multitasking*: When we're always on the go and trying to do several things simultaneously, it can be tough to slow down and appreciate the good things in life. Hectic personal schedules reduce the social touch we have with

people around us. Therefore, one can quickly cultivate poor social traits, such as ingratitude.

13. *Lack of Exposure to Diverse Perspectives*: When we only experience life from our own limited viewpoint, we may fail to appreciate the different perspectives and experiences that others can bring.

14. *Feeling Numb or Disconnected*: When we're not in touch with our emotions or feel numb or disconnected, it can be challenging to feel grateful for anything.

15. *Lack of Acknowledgment by Others*: When our efforts and accomplishments go unnoticed or unacknowledged, it can be challenging to feel grateful.

16. *Not Feeling Worthy*: It can be hard to feel grateful if we feel like we're not worthy of good things or don't deserve them.

17. *Lack of Exposure to Role Models*: Seeing others who practice gratitude can be a powerful way to learn and develop the habit ourselves. Psychology states that our positive traits are easily developed by observing our environment. The more we get

exposed to people who often display morally upright behaviors, the more often we emulate and learn such traits and make them our own.

18. *Excessive Focus on Material Possessions*: When overly focused on things and possessions, we may overlook the intangible things in life, such as relationships, experiences, and memories.

19. *Feeling Rushed or Pressured*: When we're constantly feeling rushed and pressured, we may not take the time to slow down and feel grateful for what we have.

20. *Neglecting our Spiritual or Philosophical Values:* Many religions and philosophies teach the importance of gratitude, and neglecting these values can make it harder to feel grateful.

Quotes on Ungratefulness

1. "Ingratitude is the daughter of pride." ~Miguel de Cervantes

2. "Gratitude is not only the greatest of virtues but the parent of all others." ~Marcus Tullius Cicero

3. "The greatest unhappiness comes from not being able to be grateful for what one has." ~Jean de la Bruyere

4. "Gratitude is the sign of noble souls." ~Aesop

5. "Ungratefulness is a symptom of an unhealthy soul." ~Ken Poirot

6. "Ingratitude is a crime more despicable than revenge, which is only returning evil for evil, while gratitude rises above both." ~Charles Caleb Colton

7. "Ungratefulness is a vice most unnatural." ~Timon of Athens

8. "Ungrateful people breed negativity. No one gets any pleasure from giving to an ungrateful person. When you show appreciation, the object of your attention blossoms and flourishes." ~Suze Orman

9. "Ungrateful people forget what they are not grateful for." ~Jacob Cherian

10. "An ungrateful person is like a plow horse blindly pulling." ~African Proverb

11. "Ungratefulness is worse than witchcraft." ~African Proverb

12. "Ingratitude is the essence of vileness." ~Immanuel Kant

13. "Ungratefulness is not forgetting something pleasant, but forgetting someone to whom we owe a little kindness." ~François de la Rochefoucauld

14. "Ungrateful people are never satisfied." ~James Brown

15. "Ungratefulness is a sin." ~Canada Lee

16. "A proud heart never gives thanks, for it only thinks of what it has, not what it has received." ~Thomas Kempis

17. "Ungratefulness is like a swift arrow shot from the devil's bow." ~African Proverb

18. "Ungratefulness denies the giver the joy of giving." ~Immanuel Kant

19. "Ungratefulness is a cancer that eats away at the soul;…" ~Geraldine Vermaak

20. "Ingratitude is the quickest way to lose friends." – Iranian Proverb

21. "Ungrateful people make the world miserable." ~Immanuel Kant

22. "An ungrateful person is like a tree without leaves." ~Iranian Proverb

23. "An ungrateful person is like a snake that bites the hand that feeds it." ~Michael Johns.

24. "Ungratefulness is like a thief that steals joy. It is a disease that needs a cure." ~James Lambert.

25. "An ungrateful person is like a cloud without rain." ~Arabic Proverb.

26. Ingratitude is treason to mankind." ~James Thomson.

Gratitude Quotes with References

1. "Gratitude makes sense of our past, brings peace for today, and creates a vision for tomorrow." ~Melody Beattie (Print)

2. "Gratitude is a powerful catalyst for happiness. It's the spark that lights a fire of joy in your soul." ~Amy Collette (Print)

3. "Gratitude is the healthiest of all human emotions. The more you express gratitude for what you have, the more likely you will have even more to express gratitude for." ~Zig Ziglar (Print)

4. "Gratitude unlocks the fullness of life. It turns what we have into enough and more. It turns denial into acceptance, chaos to order, confusion to clarity. It can turn a meal into a feast, a

house into a home, a stranger into a friend." ~Melody Beattie (Print)

5. "Gratitude is the fairest blossom which springs from the soul." ~Henry Ward Beecher (Print)

6. "Gratitude is when memory is stored in the heart and not in the mind." ~Lionel Hampton (Print)

7. "Gratitude is a currency that we can mint for ourselves, and spend without fear of bankruptcy." ~Fred De Witt Van Amburgh (Print)

8. "Gratitude is the most exquisite form of courtesy." ~Jacques Maritain (Print)

9. "Gratitude changes everything." ~Unknown (Print)

10. "The essence of all beautiful art, all great art, is gratitude." ~Friedrich Nietzsche (Print)

11. "When I started counting my blessings, my whole life turned around." ~Willie Nelson (Print)

12. "In ordinary life, we hardly realize that we receive a great deal more than we give and that it is only with gratitude that life becomes rich." ~Dietrich Bonhoeffer (Print)

13. "Gratitude is the memory of the heart." ~Jean Baptiste Massieu (Print)

14. "Gratitude is riches. Complaining is poverty." ~Doris Day (Print)

15. "Gratitude can transform common days into thanksgivings, turn routine jobs into joy, and change ordinary opportunities into blessings." ~William Arthur Ward (Print)

16. "Gratitude helps you to grow and expand; gratitude brings joy and laughter into your life and into the lives of all those around you." Eileen Caddy (Print)

17. "Gratitude is a quality similar to electricity: it must be produced and discharged and used up in order to exist at all." ~William Faulkner (Print)

18. "Gratitude is a powerful force that can transform your life." ~Oprah Winfrey (Print)

19. "Gratitude is one of the sweet shortcuts to finding peace of mind and happiness inside. No matter what is going on outside of us, there's always something we could be grateful for." ~Barry Neil Kaufman (Print)

20. "At times, our own light goes out and is rekindled by a spark from another person. Each of us has cause to think with deep gratitude of those who have lighted the flame within us." ~Albert Schweitzer (Print)

Examples of Ungratefulness

Ungratefulness is a subjective concept and can vary from person to person. However, ungratefulness can generally be defined as a lack of appreciation or acknowledgment for something given or done for someone. The list below provides 10 ungratefulness examples and explores the reasons behind them.

1. A child who receives a gift from their parents but complains that it's not the one they wanted. This is an example of ungratefulness because the child is not appreciating the effort and thought put into the gift by their parents.

2. An employee who receives a promotion but does not thank their boss or acknowledge the hard work of their colleagues. This is an example of ungratefulness because the employee is not recognizing the support and opportunities others provide.

3. A friend who constantly asks for favors but never returns them or expresses gratitude. This is an example of ungratefulness because the friend takes advantage of the other person's kindness without showing appreciation.

4. A student who receives a good grade on a test but complains about the difficulty of the exam. This is an example of ungratefulness because the student does not acknowledge the hard work and preparation that led to their success.

5. A spouse who receives a thoughtful gift from their partner but does not express gratitude or reciprocate with their own gift. This is an example of ungratefulness because the spouse is not valuing the effort and love put into the gift by their partner.

6. A customer who receives excellent service at a restaurant but does not leave a tip or thank the server. This is an example of ungratefulness because the customer is not recognizing the hard work and dedication of the server.

7. A celebrity who receives adoration and support from fans but does not acknowledge or appreciate their fans. This is an example of ungratefulness because the celebrity does not recognize their fans' role in their success.

8. A person who receives a life-saving organ transplant but does not thank the donor or their family. This is an example of

ungratefulness because the person does not recognize the selflessness and sacrifice of the donor and their family.

9. A politician who receives support from their constituents but does not fulfill their promises or acknowledge their supporters. This is an example of ungratefulness because the politician does not recognize the trust and faith placed in them by their constituents.

10. A pet owner who neglects or mistreats their animal despite the love and loyalty shown by the pet. This is an example of ungratefulness because the pet owner does not value their pet's companionship and devotion.

In conclusion, ungratefulness can manifest in various forms and have different underlying reasons. However, it ultimately stems from a lack of appreciation and acknowledgment for something given or done for someone. Recognizing and combatting ungratefulness in ourselves and others is vital to fostering positive relationships and a grateful attitude toward life.

The Burden of Being Ungrateful

Being ungrateful is a negative trait that can significantly burden an individual's life. It involves a lack of appreciation for the good things in one's life and a tendency to focus on the negative aspects. This can lead to feelings of dissatisfaction, unhappiness, and even depression. In this section, we will explore the burdens of being *ungrateful*.

One of the primary burdens of being ungrateful is that it can lead to a negative mindset. When someone is ungrateful, they tend to focus on what they don't have rather than what they do have. This can create a sense of dissatisfaction and unhappiness, which can be challenging to overcome. According to the Encyclopedia of Mental Health, "ungrateful people are often dissatisfied with their lives and may experience feelings of emptiness or loneliness" (Encyclopedia of Mental Health, Print).

Another burden of being ungrateful is that it can damage relationships with others. Ungrateful people may take others for granted and fail to appreciate their contributions. This can lead to resentment and conflict in relationships. The *Oxford Handbook of*

Positive Psychology notes that "ungrateful individuals are less likely to receive support from others and more likely to feel isolated and alone" (*Oxford Handbook of Positive Psychology*, Print).

A third burden of being ungrateful is that it can limit personal growth and development. When someone is ungrateful, they may fail to recognize their strengths and accomplishments. This can lead to a lack of confidence and motivation to pursue new goals. The Journal of Personality and Social Psychology explains that "ungrateful individuals are less likely to set ambitious goals for themselves and more likely to give up when faced with obstacles" (Journal of Personality and Social Psychology, Web).

Additionally, being ungrateful can negatively impact physical health. Studies have shown that ungrateful people may experience higher stress levels, which can lead to a range of health problems. As the Journal of Psychosomatic Research notes, "ungrateful individuals may be more prone to illness and disease due to the negative effects of chronic stress on the body" (Journal of Psychosomatic Research, Print).

Finally, being ungrateful can lead to a lack of empathy and compassion for others. When someone is ungrateful, they may fail to recognize the struggles and challenges that others face. This can make it difficult for them to empathize with others and offer support. The Journal of Positive Psychology explains that "ungrateful individuals are less likely to engage in prosocial behavior and more likely to exhibit negative behaviors such as aggression and hostility" (Journal of Positive Psychology, Web).

Being ungrateful is a negative trait that can significantly burden an individual's life. It can lead to a negative mindset, damage relationships, limit personal growth and development, negatively impact physical health, and lack empathy and compassion for others. Individuals need to cultivate a sense of gratitude to experience greater happiness, satisfaction, and well-being.

CHAPTER FIVE

The Psychological Ideology of Ungratefulness

Ungratefulness is a complex psychological phenomenon that has been studied extensively by psychologists. Let's explore the psychology of ungratefulness by examining its causes, effects, and potential solutions.

One of the leading causes of ungratefulness is a sense of entitlement. People who feel entitled believe that they deserve everything they receive and do not see the need to express gratitude. This sense of entitlement can be fostered by societal norms, such as the belief that success is solely the result of individual effort rather than a combination of luck, privilege, and opportunities (Algoe & Haidt, 23). Parents who overindulge their children may also contribute to their sense of entitlement, as they grow up believing that they deserve everything they want without having to work for it (Kashdan & Breen, 56).

Another cause of ungratefulness is a lack of empathy. People who cannot put themselves in others' shoes may not understand the effort or sacrifice that went into providing them with something. They may also fail to recognize the positive impact that expressing gratitude can have on others (Emmons, 34). Furthermore, people who lack empathy may be more likely to engage in self-centered behaviors, such as focusing solely on their own needs and desires rather than those of others.

Ungratefulness can have several adverse effects on both individuals and society as a whole. For individuals, ungratefulness can lead to dissatisfaction, unhappiness, and strained relationships with others (McCullough et al., 89). In extreme cases, ungratefulness can lead to a sense of entitlement and narcissism, harming one's mental health and well-being. On a societal level, ungratefulness can contribute to a lack of social cohesion and trust, as people become less likely to help others or work together towards common goals.

One potential solution to ungratefulness is practicing gratitude. Gratitude involves acknowledging the good things in one's life and expressing appreciation for them. By focusing on what they have rather than what they lack, individuals may be less likely to take things for granted and more likely to express gratitude (Wood et al., 45). Additionally, practicing gratitude has been shown to have numerous benefits, including increased happiness, improved relationships, and better physical health (Emmons & McCullough, 27).

Another potential solution to ungratefulness is developing empathy. Empathy involves understanding and sharing the feelings of others. By putting themselves in others' shoes, individuals may be more likely to recognize the effort or sacrifice that went into providing them with something and express gratitude accordingly (Kashdan & Breen, 67). Additionally, developing empathy can improve relationships with others and contribute to a sense of social cohesion.

Ungratefulness is a complex psychological phenomenon that can have negative effects on both individuals and society as a whole. It can be caused by a sense of entitlement or a lack of empathy. However, practicing gratitude and developing empathy are potential solutions that can help individuals overcome ungratefulness.

Twenty Characteristics of Ungrateful People

Ungrateful people are those who do not show appreciation or acknowledge the kindness and generosity of others. They tend to take things for granted and feel entitled to receive more without giving anything in return. Here are 20 striking characteristics of ungrateful people:

1. They don't value relationships.
2. They never say thank you.
3. They act entitled.
4. They take everything for granted.
5. They complain about what they have.
6. They criticize others for what they don't have.
7. They are never satisfied.
8. They blame others for their problems.
9. They lack empathy.
10. They don't recognize the efforts of others.
11. They don't reciprocate kindness.
12. They are selfish.
13. They are unappreciative.
14. They feel superior to others.
15. They don't apologize when they should.
16. They don't take responsibility for their actions.
17. They are disrespectful.

18. They don't listen to advice or feedback.

19. They are untrustworthy.

20. They are unreliable.

Signs of Ungratefulness

Ungratefulness is a negative trait that can manifest in various ways. It is the lack of appreciation or acknowledgment for the kindness, help, or support received from others. Recognizing the signs of ungratefulness can be crucial in maintaining healthy relationships and addressing any underlying issues. In this comprehensive response, we will explore some common signs of ungratefulness.

- *Lack of Appreciation:* One of the most evident signs of ungratefulness is a consistent lack of appreciation for the efforts made by others. This can be observed when someone fails to express gratitude or acknowledge the help they have received. They may take things for granted and not show gratitude toward those who have gone out of their way to assist them.

- *Sense of Entitlement:* Ungrateful individuals often exhibit a sense of entitlement, believing they deserve certain things without expressing gratitude or reciprocating kindness. They may expect others to cater to their needs and desires without considering the efforts made on their behalf.

- *Self-Centeredness:* Another sign of ungratefulness is excessive self-centeredness. Ungrateful individuals tend to focus solely on their own needs and desires, disregarding the feelings and efforts of others. They may fail to recognize their impact on those around them and show little empathy toward others.

- *Taking Credit for Others' Achievements*: Ungrateful people may often take credit for the accomplishments or successes resulting from collective efforts. They fail to acknowledge the contributions made by others and instead claim these achievements as their own. This behavior demonstrates a lack of gratitude towards those who have played a role in their success.

- *Negativity and Complaining*: Ungrateful individuals often display a negative attitude and constantly complain. They may focus on what they don't have rather than appreciating what they possess. This negativity can create a toxic environment and strain relationships with others.

- *Lack of Reciprocation:* Ungratefulness can also be observed when someone consistently fails to reciprocate kindness or support. They may exploit others' generosity without returning the favor or expressing gratitude. This lack of reciprocity can lead to resentment and strained relationships.

- *Disregard for Others' Feelings:* Ungrateful individuals often disregard the feelings and emotions of those around them. They may not consider how their actions or words impact others and show little empathy toward their struggles or achievements. This lack of consideration further highlights their ungrateful nature.

- *Ingratitude During Difficult Times*: Ungratefulness can become more apparent during challenging times. Instead of appreciating the support and assistance they receive, ungrateful individuals may focus on what is lacking or complain about the help they are given. This behavior demonstrates a lack of gratitude even when it is most needed.

- *Failure to Acknowledge Growth*: Ungrateful people may fail to acknowledge the personal growth or development that others have facilitated. They may not recognize the positive impact someone has had on their life, leading to a lack of appreciation for the efforts made on their behalf.

- *Lack of Thankfulness in General*: Ungratefulness can be characterized by a general lack of thankfulness in all aspects of life. Whether towards family, friends, colleagues, or even strangers, ungrateful individuals struggle to express gratitude and appreciation for the positive influences in their lives.

In closing, recognizing the signs of ungratefulness is crucial in maintaining healthy relationships and addressing any underlying issues. The signs include a lack of appreciation, a sense of entitlement, self-centeredness, taking credit for others' achievements, negativity and complaining, lack of reciprocation, disregard for others' feelings, ingratitude during difficult times, failure to acknowledge growth, and a general lack of thankfulness. By identifying these signs, individuals can work towards cultivating a more grateful and appreciative mindset.

Ungratefulness in Relationships

Ungratefulness in relationships can manifest in various ways and can be detrimental to the health of a relationship. It is the act of not showing appreciation or gratitude for the efforts, sacrifices, or love that one's partner puts into the relationship. In some cases, ungratefulness may result from taking one's partner for granted or feeling entitled to their love and affection. In other cases, it may stem from unresolved issues or resentment one partner holds towards the other. Regardless of the cause, ungratefulness can lead to feelings of hurt, frustration, and even resentment in the other partner, ultimately leading to the relationship's breakdown.

One example of ungratefulness in a relationship is when a partner fails to acknowledge or appreciate the efforts made by the other partner in maintaining the household. This can include cooking, cleaning, laundry, and other household chores often taken for granted. According to Dr. John Gottman, a renowned relationship expert and author of several books on relationships, "When partners fail to express appreciation for each other's contributions to household tasks, it can lead to feelings of resentment and disconnection" (Gottman, 56).

Another example of ungratefulness in relationships is when one partner fails to acknowledge or appreciate their partner's emotional support during difficult times. In her book *The Seven Principles for Making Marriage Work*, Dr. Julie Gottman explains that "emotional support is critical to maintaining a healthy relationship" (Gottman, 78). When one partner fails to acknowledge or appreciate their partner's emotional support during difficult times such as illness or job loss, it can lead to feelings of isolation and disconnection.

A third example of ungratefulness in relationships is when one partner fails to acknowledge or appreciate their partner's efforts to improve themselves. This can include improving their physical health, career goals, or personal development. According to Dr. Harriet Lerner, author of *The Dance of Anger*, "When partners fail to acknowledge or appreciate their partner's efforts to improve themselves, it can lead to feelings of resentment and disconnection" (Lerner, 92).

A fourth example of ungratefulness in relationships is when one partner fails to acknowledge or appreciate their partner's efforts to maintain intimacy and romance. This can include planning date nights, expressing affection, and engaging in physical intimacy. According to Dr. Sue Johnson, author of *Hold Me Tight*, "When partners fail to acknowledge or appreciate each other's efforts to maintain intimacy and romance, it can lead to feelings of loneliness and disconnection" (Johnson, 107).

Finally, a fifth example of ungratefulness in relationships is when one partner consistently criticizes or belittles the other partner's efforts. This can include criticism about their appearance, career goals, or personal interests. According to Dr. Brené Brown, author of *The Gifts of Imperfection*, "When partners consistently criticize or belittle each other's efforts, it can lead to feelings of shame and disconnection" (Brown,74).

To wrap it up, ungratefulness in relationships can manifest in various ways and be detrimental to the health of a relationship. Partners must express appreciation and gratitude for each other's efforts, sacrifices, and love to maintain a healthy and fulfilling relationship.

Ungratefulness in the Workplace

Ungratefulness is a common problem in many workplaces. It can be defined as the lack of appreciation or acknowledgment for the efforts and contributions made by others. Ungratefulness can manifest in various ways, such as failing to say thank you, taking credit for someone else's work, or not acknowledging the efforts of others. This behavior can harm morale, motivation, and productivity in the workplace.

A lack of communication is one of the leading causes of ungratefulness in the workplace. When employees do not communicate effectively with each other, it can lead to misunderstandings and misinterpretations of intentions. This can result in employees feeling undervalued and unappreciated, which can cause resentment and lead to ungrateful behavior.

Another cause of ungratefulness is a lack of recognition for achievements. Employees who feel that their hard work and efforts go unnoticed are more likely to become resentful and ungrateful. This can be particularly true when they see others receiving recognition for similar or lesser achievements.

Ungratefulness can also be caused by a toxic work environment. A culture of negativity, blame-shifting, and backstabbing can create an atmosphere where people are less likely to appreciate the contributions of others.

The effects of ungratefulness in the workplace can be significant. It can lead to decreased morale, lower job satisfaction, and reduced productivity. It can also contribute to higher levels of stress and burnout among employees.

Employers must create a culture of appreciation and recognition to address ungratefulness in the workplace. This can be done through regular feedback sessions, public recognition of achievements, and offering incentives for outstanding performance. Employers should also encourage open communication between employees and provide opportunities for team-building activities.

Ungratefulness in the workplace is a significant problem that can have a negative impact on morale, motivation, and productivity. It can be caused by a lack of communication, a lack of recognition for achievements, and a toxic work environment. To address this issue, employers should create a culture of appreciation and recognition, encourage open communication between employees, and provide opportunities for team-building activities.

The Spiritual Interpretation of Ungratefulness

The spiritual ideology of lack of gratitude is a belief system that revolves around the idea that one should not be grateful for what they have but instead focus on what they do not have. This ideology is often associated with a sense of entitlement and a lack of appreciation for the blessings in one's life. Those who subscribe to this ideology may find themselves constantly seeking more, never satisfied with what they have, and always looking for something better.

One of the critical aspects of the lack of gratitude ideology is the belief that one is entitled to certain things in life, such as success, wealth, and happiness. This entitlement can lead to a sense of dissatisfaction with one's current situation, as they may feel that they are not getting what they deserve. This can create a negative cycle in which the individual becomes increasingly focused on their lack rather than appreciating what they have.

Another aspect of the lack of gratitude ideology is the belief that success and happiness are solely determined by external factors, such as wealth or status. Those who subscribe to this ideology may believe they would be happier and more successful if they had more money or a higher social status. This can lead to constant searching for external validation and never being satisfied with one's current situation.

The lack of gratitude ideology can also manifest itself in relationships. Those who believe in this ideology may feel that their partner or friends are not doing enough for them and may constantly seek more attention or validation from others. This can create a sense of tension and dissatisfaction in relationships, as others may feel that their efforts are not appreciated or valued.

Ultimately, the lack of gratitude ideology can lead to a sense of emptiness and unhappiness. By focusing solely on what one does not have rather than appreciating what one possesses, individuals may find themselves constantly searching for something more. This can create a sense of restlessness and dissatisfaction that can be difficult to overcome.

In summary, the spiritual ideology of lack of gratitude is a belief system that can negatively impact an individual's life. By focusing solely on what one does not have, rather than appreciating what they do have, individuals may find themselves constantly searching for something more. This can create a sense of entitlement and dissatisfaction that can be difficult to overcome.

Ways of Dealing with Ungrateful People

Dealing with ungrateful people can be challenging, but there are various ways to handle such situations. According to publications, some of the ways to deal with ungrateful people are:

1. _Set boundaries:_ Establish clear boundaries to protect yourself from being taken advantage of or mistreated. Clearly and respectfully communicate your expectations and limits.

2. _Practice self-care_: Prioritize self-care to ensure you have the emotional resilience to deal with ungrateful people. Engage in activities that bring you joy, relaxation, and rejuvenation.

3. _Avoid taking it personally_: Remember that someone's ungratefulness is often a reflection of their own issues rather than a reflection of your worth or actions. Don't internalize their behavior.

4. _Focus on gratitude_: Cultivate a mindset of gratitude in your own life. By focusing on the positive aspects of your

experiences, you can counterbalance the negativity of ungrateful people.

5. *Communicate assertively*: When dealing with ungrateful individuals, express your feelings and concerns assertively but respectfully. Use "I" statements to convey how their behavior affects you without blaming or attacking them.

6. *Practice active listening*: When conversing with ungrateful people, practice active listening by giving them your full attention and validating their feelings. This can help defuse tension and foster better communication.

7. *Offer constructive feedback*: If appropriate, provide constructive feedback to the ungrateful person about their behavior. Frame it in a way that focuses on the impact of their actions rather than criticizing them personally.

8. *Seek support:* Reach out to trusted friends, family members, or professionals for support and guidance when dealing with ungrateful people. They can provide valuable insights and help you navigate challenging situations.

9. *Avoid enabling*: Refrain from enabling ungrateful behavior by constantly rescuing or accommodating the person's demands. Encourage them to take responsibility for their actions and consequences.

10. *Practice forgiveness:* Let go of resentment and practice forgiveness towards ungrateful individuals. Holding onto anger or grudges only harms your own well-being.

11. *Redirect the conversation*: If a conversation with an ungrateful person becomes toxic or unproductive, redirect the topic to something more positive or neutral. This can help diffuse tension and maintain a healthier interaction.

12. *Lead by example*: Demonstrate gratitude and appreciation in your actions and interactions. You may inspire others to adopt a more grateful mindset by modeling gratitude.

13. *Avoid escalating conflicts*: Recognize when a situation becomes too heated or unproductive and take steps to de-escalate conflicts. This may involve taking a break, changing the subject, or seeking necessary mediation.

14. *Practice patience*: Dealing with ungrateful people requires patience and understanding. Recognize that change takes time, and not everyone may be receptive to your efforts immediately.

15. *Focus on the positive impact*: Instead of dwelling on the negativity of ungrateful people, focus on the positive impact you can have on others who appreciate your efforts and kindness.

16. *Accept limitations*: You cannot control how others behave or feel. Accepting this reality can help you let go of frustration and focus on what you can control – your own reactions and choices.

17. *Seek professional help if needed*: If dealing with ungrateful people becomes overwhelming or affects your mental well-being, consider seeking professional help from therapists or counselors specializing in interpersonal relationships.

18. *Practice empathy*: Try to put yourself in the shoes of the ungrateful person and understand their perspective. This can

help you approach the situation with compassion and find common ground.

19. *Let go when necessary*: If all efforts to deal with ungrateful people prove futile and continue to negatively impact your well-being, it may be necessary to distance yourself from them. Sometimes, letting go is the healthiest choice for your happiness and peace of mind.

Disadvantages of being Ungrateful

Being ungrateful can have numerous negative consequences. Here are 20 disadvantages of being ungrateful:

1. *Unhappiness:* One of the primary disadvantages of being ungrateful is that it often leads to unhappiness. When individuals fail to appreciate the positive aspects of their lives, they focus on what they lack or what goes wrong, leading to constant dissatisfaction.

2. *Strained Relationships*: Ungratefulness can strain relationships with friends, family, and colleagues. Ungrateful people often fail to acknowledge the efforts and support provided by others, leading to resentment and distance in relationships.

3. *Lack of Contentment*: Gratitude promotes contentment and acceptance of one's circumstances. Conversely, being ungrateful fosters a constant desire for more or better things, making it difficult to find satisfaction in what one already has.

4. *Decreased Well-Being*: Studies have shown that gratitude is associated with increased well-being and positive emotions. On the other hand, being ungrateful can contribute to feelings of negativity, stress, and anxiety.

5. *Limited Perspective*: Ungrateful individuals tend to have a limited perspective on life. They may overlook the positive aspects of their experiences and focus solely on the negative, which can hinder personal growth and resilience.

6. *Inability to Enjoy the Present Moment*: Being ungrateful often prevents individuals from thoroughly enjoying and savoring the present moment. Instead of appreciating the here and now, they may constantly seek something better or dwell on past disappointments.

7. *Lack of Empathy:* Gratitude is closely linked to empathy and compassion. When individuals are ungrateful, they may struggle to understand and empathize with the experiences and feelings of others, leading to strained relationships and a lack of emotional connection.

8. *Increased Stress Levels*: Ungratefulness can contribute to higher stress levels. Constantly focusing on what is lacking or what went wrong can create a negative mindset that perpetuates stress and anxiety.

9. *Decreased Resilience*: Gratitude has been found to enhance resilience, helping individuals bounce back from adversity. Conversely, being ungrateful can make coping with setbacks and obstacles more challenging, as the focus remains on the negative rather than finding solutions.

10. *Impaired Mental Health*: Research suggests that gratitude is associated with improved mental health outcomes, such as reduced symptoms of depression and increased life satisfaction. In contrast, being ungrateful can contribute to developing or exacerbating mental health issues.

11. *Lack of Motivation*: Ungrateful individuals may struggle with motivation as they fail to appreciate their progress or the opportunities available to them. This lack of motivation can hinder personal growth and achievement.

12. *Negative Impact on Self-Esteem*: Being ungrateful often leads to a negative self-perception. Individuals may compare themselves unfavorably to others or focus on their perceived shortcomings, leading to lower self-esteem and confidence.

13. *Missed Growth Opportunities*: Gratitude allows individuals to recognize and learn from their experiences, even those that may initially seem negative. By being ungrateful, individuals may miss out on valuable lessons and personal growth opportunities.

14. *Difficulty in Forming Meaningful Connections*: Ungratefulness can make forming deep and meaningful connections with others challenging. People are naturally drawn to those who appreciate and acknowledge their efforts, making it harder for ungrateful individuals to build strong relationships.

15. *Reduced Productivity*: A lack of gratitude can negatively impact productivity levels. When individuals fail to recognize and appreciate the resources and support available, they may not fully utilize their potential or take advantage of opportunities.

16. *Increased Feelings of Entitlement*: Ungratefulness often leads to a sense of entitlement, where individuals believe they deserve more without putting in the necessary effort. This entitlement mindset can hinder personal growth and lead to strained relationships with others.

17. *Lack of Resilience in the Face of Adversity*: Gratitude has been linked to increased resilience, allowing individuals to navigate challenges and setbacks more effectively.

Conversely, being ungrateful can make it harder to bounce back from adversity and find the strength to persevere.

18. *Negative Impact on Physical Health*: Research suggests that gratitude is associated with improved physical health outcomes, such as better sleep quality and reduced symptoms of illness. On the other hand, being ungrateful can contribute to increased stress levels and compromised physical well-being.

19. *Missed Opportunities for Joy*: Gratitude allows individuals to find joy in everyday experiences and appreciate the small moments of happiness. By being ungrateful, individuals may overlook these opportunities for joy, leading to a less fulfilling life.

20. *Lack of Personal Fulfillment*: Ultimately, being ungrateful can prevent individuals from experiencing a sense of personal fulfillment and satisfaction. Without gratitude, it becomes challenging to find meaning and purpose in life.

In closing, being ungrateful can have numerous negative consequences. Firstly, it can damage relationships with family, friends, and colleagues. Ungrateful people often take others for granted and fail to appreciate their efforts and contributions, leading to resentment and conflict. Secondly, ungrateful people tend to have a negative attitude towards life, focusing on what they lack rather than what they have. This can lead to feelings of dissatisfaction and unhappiness. Finally, ungrateful people may struggle to develop meaningful connections with others as their self-centered behavior can be off-putting.

Advantages of Gratitude

Gratitude is a powerful emotion that can positively affect an individual's life. Here are some advantages of gratitude:

1. *Improves Physical Health*: Grateful people ultimately have mental and physiological aspects of the body balanced, which are critical for physical health. Gratitude has been associated with lower blood pressure, reduced inflammation, and stronger immune function.

2. *Enhances Psychological Well-Being*: Psychologists believe that gratefulness stimulates certain body hormones that trigger peaceful body conditions.

3. *Reduces Stress*: Holding onto ungrateful emotions about a person or a group of people is just like holding onto hatred. The moment one lets go of ungratefulness, they relieve themselves of stress. Being grateful helps to counteract stress and promotes relaxation.

4. *Increases Resilience*: Ungratefulness increases personal endurance to daily life challenges as they readily accept the

unfolding of life as it happens, whether satisfactory or unsatisfactory. Grateful people are better equipped to handle challenges and bounce back from adversity.

5. *Improved Mental Health*: Gratitude has been linked to reduced symptoms of depression and anxiety.

6. *Enhanced Emotional Well-Being*: Gratitude promotes positive emotions such as joy, love, happiness, and contentment.

7. *Enhanced Self-Esteem*: Grateful individuals tend to have higher self-worth and confidence.

8. *Strengthened Relationships*: Gratitude fosters positive social connections and deepens bonds with others.

9. *Better Sleep Quality*: Practicing gratitude before bed can improve sleep duration and quality.

10. *Enhanced Empathy*: Gratitude cultivates compassion and empathy towards others.

11. *Increased Optimism*: Grateful individuals tend to have a more positive outlook.

12. *Boosted Motivation*: Expressing gratitude can increase motivation and drive towards achieving goals.

13. *Improved Decision-Making*: Gratitude enhances cognitive function, leading to better decision-making abilities.

14. *Greater Satisfaction with Life*: Practicing gratitude helps individuals appreciate what they have, leading to greater overall life satisfaction.

15. *Increased Productivity*: Grateful people are more focused, motivated, and productive in their daily lives.

16. *Enhanced Emotional Intelligence*: Gratitude promotes emotional awareness and regulation.

17. *Improved physical fitness*: Grateful individuals are more likely to exercise regularly and take care of their physical health.

18. *Reduced Materialism*: Gratitude shifts the focus from material possessions to appreciating experiences and relationships.

19. *Increased Generosity*: Grateful individuals are likelier to act kindly and help others.

20. *Improved Problem-Solving Skills*: Gratitude enhances cognitive flexibility and creativity, leading to better problem-solving abilities.

21. *Enhanced Mindfulness*: Practicing gratitude encourages being present in the moment and savoring positive experiences.

22. *Increased Resilience to Trauma*: Gratitude can help individuals cope with traumatic events and facilitate post-traumatic growth.

23. *Improved Work Satisfaction*: Expressing gratitude fosters a positive work environment and increases job satisfaction.

24. *Increased social support*: Grateful individuals tend to have stronger social networks and receive more support from others.

25. *Overall Improved Quality of Life*: Regularly practicing gratitude leads to a more fulfilling and meaningful life.

More Readings About Gratitude

Ungratefulness is a common human trait that can often lead to dissatisfaction and unhappiness. To understand this concept better, several published books provide insights into ungrateful people and their behavior. One such book is _The Narcissism Epidemic: Living in the Age of Entitlement_ by Jean M. Twenge and W. Keith Campbell (Print), which explains how narcissism and entitlement can lead to ungrateful behavior. Another book, _The Gratitude Diaries: How a Year Looking on the Bright Side Can Transform Your Life_ by Janice Kaplan (Print), explores the benefits of gratitude and how it can counteract ungratefulness.

In _The Power of Gratitude: 21 Verses of Thanks to Inspire Peace and Joy_ by Ruth Ward (Print), the author provides inspirational quotes and verses encouraging gratitude to combat ungratefulness. Similarly, _The Little Book of Gratitude: Create a Life of Happiness and Wellbeing by Giving Thanks_ by Dr. Robert A. Emmons (Print) offers practical tips for cultivating gratitude daily.

Finally, _The Art of Happiness_ by the Dalai Lama and Howard C. Cutler (Print) discusses the role of gratitude in achieving happiness and fulfillment in life, emphasizing the importance of recognizing and appreciating the good things we have.

These print sources provide valuable insights into ungrateful behavior, its causes, and life-changing ways to combat it through gratitude.

CHAPTER SIX

Checks and Therapy

The Importance of Teaching Gratitude Among Children

G ratitude is an essential virtue that can be taught to children from a young age. It is the act of being thankful and appreciative of the good things in life, no matter how small they may seem. Teaching gratitude to children has numerous benefits that can positively impact their mental health, social skills, and overall well-being.

One of the most significant benefits of teaching gratitude to children is that it helps them develop a positive attitude toward life. When children learn to appreciate the good things in their lives, they are less likely to focus on the negative aspects. This positive attitude can help them cope with difficult situations and challenges they may face. According to a study published in the *Journal of Positive*

Psychology, individuals who practice gratitude have higher happiness and life satisfaction levels.

Teaching gratitude also helps children develop empathy and compassion towards others. When children learn to appreciate what they have, they are more likely to understand and empathize with those who may be less fortunate. This empathy can help them form stronger relationships with others and become more socially aware. A study conducted by researchers at Northeastern University found that individuals who practice gratitude are more likely to exhibit prosocial behavior.

Furthermore, teaching gratitude can help children develop resilience and emotional regulation skills. When children learn to focus on the positive aspects of their lives, they are better equipped to handle stress and adversity. Gratitude can also help children regulate their emotions by encouraging them to focus on positive thoughts and feelings. According to a study published in the *Journal of School Psychology*, students who practiced gratitude had lower levels of depression and anxiety.

Another benefit of teaching gratitude is that it can improve academic performance. When children are grateful for their education and opportunities, they are more motivated to learn and achieve their goals. Gratitude can also help children develop a growth mindset, which is the belief that their abilities can improve with effort and practice. A study published in the *Journal of Happiness Studies* found that students who practiced gratitude had higher levels of academic achievement.

Finally, teaching gratitude can help children develop a sense of purpose and meaning in their lives. When children learn to appreciate the good things in their lives, they are more likely to feel a sense of fulfillment and purpose. Gratitude can also help children develop a deeper understanding of their values and beliefs. According to a study published in the *Journal of Positive Psychology*, individuals who practice gratitude have a stronger sense of meaning and purpose in life.

Teaching gratitude to children has numerous benefits that can positively impact their mental health, social skills, academic performance, and overall well-being. By encouraging children to appreciate the good things in their lives, we can help them develop a positive attitude, empathy and compassion towards others, resilience and emotional regulation skills, academic motivation and achievement, and a sense of purpose and meaning.

Overcoming the Feeling of Entitlement

Entitlement is a feeling of deserving something without having to work for it. It is a common problem that many people face in their lives. Entitlement can lead to dissatisfaction, frustration, and disappointment in oneself and others. It is essential to overcome feelings of entitlement to live a fulfilling life. Here are some ways to overcome feelings of entitlement.

- *Gratitude:* Gratitude is the opposite of entitlement. Feeling grateful for what you have makes you less likely to feel entitled. Practice gratitude by listing things you are thankful for each day. This will help you focus on the positive things in your life rather than what you think you deserve.

- *Hard work:* Entitlement often comes from a belief that things should be easy and come naturally. However, this is not always the case. Hard work is necessary to achieve success in life. By putting in the effort and working hard, you will feel a sense of accomplishment and pride in your achievements.

- *Perspective:* Sometimes, entitlement can come from a lack of perspective. It is important to remember that everyone has struggles and challenges. By putting yourself in someone else's shoes, you can better understand their situation and develop empathy.

- *Humility:* Humility is the opposite of entitlement. When you are humble, you acknowledge that you are not perfect and that there is always room for improvement. By being humble, you can learn from others and grow as a person.

- *Focus on others:* Entitlement often comes from a focus on oneself. By shifting your focus to others, you can develop empathy and compassion for those around you. Volunteer your time or donate to charity to help those in need.

Overcoming feelings of entitlement requires a shift in mindset and perspective. By practicing gratitude, working hard, gaining perspective, being humble, and focusing on others, you can overcome feelings of entitlement and live a fulfilling life.

Cultivating Gratefulness Mindset

Cultivating a gratefulness mindset is an essential aspect of leading a fulfilling life. Gratefulness is the ability to appreciate the good things in life, no matter how small they may be. It is an attitude that can help us find joy and contentment in our daily lives. In this section, we will explore how to cultivate a gratefulness mindset.

- *Practice Mindfulness:* Mindfulness is the practice of being present in the moment. It involves paying attention to your thoughts, feelings, and surroundings without judgment. Mindfulness can help you appreciate the small things in life that you may have otherwise overlooked. For example, you may start to notice the beauty of nature or the kindness of strangers.

- *Keep a Gratitude Journal:* A gratitude journal is a powerful way to cultivate a gratefulness mindset. Each day, write down three things that you are grateful for. They can be as simple as having a roof over your head or as significant as achieving a personal goal. Focusing on the positive aspects of your life can help you feel more content and appreciative.

- *Practice Self-Compassion:* Self-compassion is the practice of treating yourself with kindness and understanding. It involves acknowledging your flaws and mistakes without judgment or criticism. When you practice self-compassion, you can learn to appreciate yourself for who you are rather than focusing on what you lack.

Expressing Your Gratitude

Expressing gratitude to others can also help cultivate a gratitude mindset. Take the time to thank someone who has helped you or positively impacted your life. You can write them a note, email them, or tell them in person. Expressing your gratitude helps you feel more appreciative and strengthens your relationships with others. My overall advice is to try and impact someone positively with kind words of encouragement.

Surrounding Yourself with Positivity

Surrounding yourself with positivity can also help cultivate a gratitude mindset. Spend time with people who uplift and inspire you. Read books or watch movies that make you feel good. Listen to music that brings you joy. When you surround yourself with positivity, you are more likely to focus on the good things in life.

CHAPTER SEVEN

Consider It For the Better

As read in the previous three chapters, ungratefulness is not a positive character trait. Even after Jimmy reluctantly read the note Lizzy handed him, he was still not moved. It took Lizzy three years to work on Jimmy to see if he would improve his lack of gratitude trait but to no avail. Unfortunately, Jimmy continuously felt the world belonged to him by believing and selfishly acting like the world was his. He was entitled to whatever job he requested, with the conditions Jimmy wanted and the desired pay.

Those who knew Lizzy in the neighborhood as a Good Samaritan advised her to get rid of Jimmy due to his bold, ungrateful behavior. However, with her humble nature, Lizzy kept working on Jimmy's attitude to see if she could generally transform his perception of life. She kept helping him emotionally and financially, whatever it would take to get him back on track.

Nevertheless, sometimes, to find what you appreciate in life, you need to list what you don't appreciate or are not thankful for. The benefit of this is that it helps you separate the stuff you actually do not appreciate from the things you happen to be losing interest in because of the act of ingratitude. You need to help others by telling yourself the truth and encouraging yourself to cultivate gratitude. If you are ungrateful, this part will be hard because your ungratefulness will try to pull you back to social isolation. However, social isolation has proven time and time again to be bad for our health. Humans are social creatures, and whether you're an extrovert or an introvert, you need regular social contact to stay healthy, speak to people happily, and always have a reason to appreciate them.

Try to consciously connect with the people you love, a support group, neighbors, religious group, or trusted friends. Do not relate with them with any expectation of any result; focus on positively being with them. The guilt that comes with ungratefulness can sometimes lead to self-deprecation. We all have events in our lives that we wish had gone differently. Still, your ingratitude can make these events play over and over again in your memory and make you feel you are doing the right thing. To help you navigate this negative process, remember when someone was kind to you and made you happy, granting you your wishes even when you were not expecting it. Maybe someone complimented you when they were not obligated to do so, or an advisor, counselor, or teacher helped you when you were struggling. If you can find things that make you feel a little more content, that will help you start being grateful. However, gratitude can help to ease unfavorable thought processes and degrade manifestations and symptoms so you can improve your well-being concerning gratitude. I advise you to experiment with ways to show gratitude daily and find the best method for you.

In conclusion, ungratefulness is a detrimental attitude that can have adverse effects on individuals and society as a whole. It is the failure to appreciate or acknowledge the kindness, help, or benefits received from others. Ungratefulness often stems from entitlement, selfishness, or a lack of empathy. It can lead to strained relationships, decreased well-being, and a breakdown in social cohesion.

One of the main consequences of ungratefulness is the strain it puts on relationships. When someone consistently fails to express gratitude for the efforts and support others provide, it can create resentment and frustration. This can lead to a breakdown in communication and trust, ultimately damaging the bond between individuals. Ungratefulness can erode the love and affection that once existed in personal relationships, causing emotional distance and potential separation. In professional settings, ungratefulness can harm teamwork and collaboration, hindering productivity and success.

Furthermore, ungratefulness has a direct impact on an individual's well-being. Gratitude has been shown to have numerous psychological and physical benefits, such as increased happiness, improved mental health, better sleep quality, and reduced stress levels. Conversely, ungratefulness can contribute to dissatisfaction, resentment, and unhappiness. It creates a negative mindset that focuses on what is lacking rather than appreciating what one already has. This constant dissatisfaction can lead to a perpetual cycle of seeking more without ever finding true fulfillment.

On a broader scale, ungratefulness can have detrimental effects on society. A lack of gratitude undermines social cohesion and fosters an environment of entitlement and self-centeredness. When individuals fail to recognize the contributions made by others or take them for granted, it diminishes the motivation for acts of kindness and generosity. This can lead to a breakdown in community spirit and cooperation. In contrast, gratitude promotes prosocial behavior and strengthens social bonds by fostering a sense of interconnectedness and mutual support.

Addressing ungratefulness requires a shift in mindset and the cultivation of gratitude. It is important to recognize and appreciate the efforts and contributions of others, no matter how small. Expressing gratitude benefits the recipient and enhances the well-being of the person expressing it. Simple acts such as saying "thank you," writing thank-you notes, or performing acts of kindness can go a long way in fostering a culture of gratitude.

Lastly, ungratefulness is a destructive attitude that can have far-reaching consequences. It strains relationships, diminishes well-being, and undermines social cohesion. Cultivating gratitude is essential for personal growth, healthy relationships, and a thriving society. By recognizing and appreciating the kindness and support we receive from others, we can foster a culture of gratitude that promotes happiness, fulfillment, and harmonious coexistence.

Cultivating a gratefulness mindset can have a profound impact on your life. By practicing mindfulness, keeping a gratitude journal, practicing self-compassion, expressing your gratitude, and surrounding yourself with positivity, you can learn to appreciate the good things in life and find joy in the present moment. The worst reputation for an ungrateful person is when they have received more than they can handle and still cannot say thank you. Don't let this be said about you.

REFERENCES

Alberti, R. E., & Emmons, M. L. (2017). *Your Perfect Right: Assertiveness and Equality in Your Life and Relationships.* Impact Publishers

Algoe, S. B., Gable, S. L., & Maisel, N. C. (2010). *It's the little things: Everyday gratitude as a booster shot for romantic relationships.* Personal Relationships, 17(2), 217-233. (Print)

Brown, B. (2010). *The Gifts of Imperfection: Let Go of Who You Think You're Supposed to Be and Embrace Who You Are.* Hazelden Publishing.

Carnegie, D. (2004). *How to Stop Worrying and Start Living.* Simon and Schuster.

Cloud, H., & Townsend, J. (2017). *Boundaries: When to Say Yes, How to Say No To Take Control of Your Life.* Zondervan.

Dalai Lama, & Cutler, H. C. (1998). *The Art of Happiness*. Riverhead Books.

Davis, D. E., Choe, E., Meyers, J., Wade, N., Varjas, K., Gifford, A., ... & Worthington Jr, E. L. (2016). Thankful for the little things: A meta-analysis of gratitude interventions. *Journal of Counseling Psychology*, 63(1), 20-31. (Print)

Dweck, C. S. (2006). *Mindset: The New Psychology of Success*. Random House Digital, Inc. (Print)

Emmons, Robert A., and Michael E. McCullough. "Counting blessings versus burdens: An experimental investigation of gratitude and subjective well-being in daily life." *Journal of Personality and Social Psychology* 84.2 (2003): 377-389. (Print)

Hill, P.L., Allemand, M., Roberts, B.W., Lodi-Smith, J., & Costa Jr, P.T. (2013). Examining the pathways between gratitude and self-rated physical health across adulthood. *Personality and Individual Differences*, 54(1), 92-96. (Print)

Kaplan, J. (2015). *The Gratitude Diaries: How a Year Looking on the Bright Side Can Transform Your Life*. Dutton.

Kashdan, Todd B., and Jason R. Breen. "Materialism and diminished well-being: Experiential avoidance as a mediating mechanism." *Journal of Social and Clinical Psychology* 26.5 (2007): 521-539. (Print)

Kassin, S., Fein, S., & Markus, H.R. (2014). *Social Psychology (9th ed.)*. Cengage Learning (Print).

Kyeong, S., Kim, J. H., & Lee, H. K. (2016). The Effects of Mindfulness Meditation on Empathy and Burnout in Medical Residents. *Journal of Korean Medical Science*, 31(12), 1955-1960. (Print)

Lambert, N.M., Fincham, F.D., & Stillman, T.F. (2010). Gratitude and depressive symptoms: The role of positive reframing and positive emotion. *Cognition and Emotion*, 24(3), 387-400. (Print)

McCullough, Michael E., et al. "Gratitude and prosocial behavior: Helping when it costs you." *Psychological Science* 17.4 (2006): 319-325. (Print)

Seligman, M.E.P (2011). *Flourish: A Visionary New Understanding of Happiness and Well-Being.* New York: Free Press. (Print)

Seligman, M.E.P., & Csikszentmihalyi, M. (2000). *Positive Psychology: An Introduction* (pp 279-298). American Psychological Association (Print).

Tolle, E. (1999). *The Power of Now: A Guide to Spiritual Enlightenment.* New World Library. (Print)

Twenge, J.M., Konrath, S., Foster, J.D., Campbell, W.K., & Bushman, B.J. (2014). Egos inflating over time: A cross-temporal meta-analysis of the Narcissistic Personality Inventory. *Journal of Personality*, 76(4), 875-902. (Print)

Ward, R. (2017). *The Power of Gratitude: 21 Verses of Thanks to Inspire Peace and Joy.* CreateSpace Independent Publishing Platform.

Watkins, P.C., Woodward, K., Stone, T., & Kolts, R.L. (2003).
Gratitude and happiness: Development of a measure of
gratitude and relationships with subjective well-being. *Social
Behavior and Personality: An International Journal*, 31(5),
431-451. (Print)

Wood, A.M., Joseph, S., & Maltby, J. (2009). Gratitude Predicts
Psychological Well-Being Above the Big Five Facets
(Personality and Individual Differences, Vol 46(4), pp 443-
447 (Print).

WORKBOOK A

Listed below are 20 behaviors and typical features that are natural among human beings. Review these typical features and answer True or False by checking the one that best describes you.

1. Do you value relationships? Yes   or No

2. Do you say thank you when someone favors you?   Yes   or No

3. Do you act entitled?   Yes   or   No

4. Do you take everything for granted? Yes   or No

5. Do you complain about what you have? Yes   or   No

6. Do you criticize others for what they don't have? Yes   or   No

7. Are you ever satisfied with what you have?   Yes   or   No

8. Do you blame others for your problems?   Yes   or   No

9. Do you lack empathy? Yes   or   No

10. Do you recognize the efforts of others? Yes   or   No

11. Do you reciprocate kindness?   Yes   or   No

12. Do you think you are selfish?   Yes   or   No

13. Do you think you are unappreciative?   Yes   or   No

14. Do you think you are superior to others?   Yes   or   No

15. Do you apologize when you offend people?   Yes   or   No

16. Do you take responsibility for your actions?   Yes   or   No

17. Do you think you are sometimes disrespectful?   Yes   or   No

18. Do you listen to advice or feedback from others?   Yes   or   No

19. Are you trustworthy, dependable, and responsible?   Yes   or   No

20. Are you reliable, steadfast and dedicated toward positivity?

Yes   or   No

WORKBOOK B

1. Describe the event and identify specific things someone said or did that brought on your ingratitude.

_____

_____

_____

_____

_____

_____

_____

_____

_____

_____

_____

_____

_____

2. **List out any emotions that were basically your feelings on gratitude.**

_____

_____

_____

_____

_____

_____

_____

_____

_____

_____

_____

_____

_____

_____

_____

_____

3. **What do you constantly do to make others happy or feel better?**

_____

_____

_____

_____

_____

_____

_____

_____

_____

_____

_____

_____

_____

_____

_____

4. **What do you need someone else to do to help you feel better?**

_____

_____

_____

_____

_____

_____

_____

_____

_____

_____

_____

_____

_____

5. **Describe the event or identify specific things someone said or did that brought on your ingratitude to the scenario.**

_____

_____

_____

_____

_____

_____

_____

_____

_____

_____

_____

_____

_____

_____

WORKBOOK C

Circle the option that best describes you.

1. How often do you make a request for financial or material things?

   A. Daily   B. Weekly   C. Monthly   D. Yearly

   E. Rarely

2. When we are not actively grateful, we leave space for discontent to flourish.   True or False

3. We may push friends, family, or co-workers away if ingratitude makes us negative.   True or False

4. When we are ungrateful, we tend to miss out on life's beauty.   True or False

5. Gratitude can help to balance issues. Without gratitude, the negative takes hold of our attention. True or False

6. Gratitude can help you to experience more positive emotions.   True or False

7. Gratitude can improve relationships, building new ones and strengthening current ones.   True or False

8. Gratitude predicts less anxiety, recession, and panic symptoms.   True   or   False

9. Expressing appreciation may train the brain to be more sensitive to the experience of gratitude for a period of time.

True   or   False

10. Gratitude may increase self-esteem and may help to boost resilience.   True   or   False

WORKBOOK D

Listed below are 10 behaviors and typical natural features among ungrateful people. Review these typical features and check if they reflect you most often, sometimes, or hardly. Using numbers" Most Often as 1, Sometimes as 2, or Hardly as 3. *(NOTE: Judge sincerely.)*

	Most Often	Sometimes	Hardly
1. How often do you do one nice thing for someone, and expect ten in return. 6?			
2. Do you perceive ungratefulness is linked to selfishness?			
3. Do you think there are multiple causes associated with ungrateful behavior?			
4. Do you believe an ungrateful person is egoistic?			
5. Do you think an ungrateful individual needs a change of attitude or not?			

6. Do you think showing gratitude is necessary?			
7. How often do you give other people your time out of the goodness of your heart?			
8. Do you think you only have to be thankful for the biggest things someone does for you?			
9. How often do you ever hold yourself accountable for your mistakes?			
10. How often do you tend to be emotionally unstable?			

Exercise: For every sentence that applies to you, score yourself 2 points for "Most of the time," 1 point for "sometimes," and no points for "Hardly" response. The higher your score means you definitely need to work on yourself.

Your Score: _____

WORKBOOK E

Listed below are 10 behaviors and typical natural features among ungrateful people. Review these typical features and check if they reflect you most often, sometimes, or hardly. Using numbers: Most Often as 1, Sometimes as 2, or Hardly as 3.
(NOTE: Judge sincerely.)

	Most Often	Sometimes	Hardly
1. How often do you remember people who have positively impacted your life?			
2. Do you appreciate the valuable things you have, and how often are you happy to have them?			
3. How often do you reflect respect and dignity toward others?			
4. How often do you stay calm when your request for assistance doesn't get to you at your own pace?			
5. How often do you take advantage of other people's kindness?			

6. How often do you give yourself credit for getting through an uncomfortable situation?			
7. How often do you have an entitled attitude?			
8. How often do you blame others for your problem?			
9. How often do you have a victim mentality?			
10. How often do you have misunderstandings with people?			

Exercise: For every sentence that applies to you, score yourself 2 points for "Most of the time," 1 point for "sometimes," and no points for "Hardly" response. The higher your score means you definitely need to work on yourself.

Your Score: _____

WORKBOOK F

1. **What's the number one thing you wish more people knew about you?**

   _____

   _____

   _____

   _____

   _____

   _____

   _____

   _____

2. **Has a random stranger ever made a tremendous impact on you, and how do you feel about it?**

   _____

   _____

   _____

   _____

   _____

   _____

   _____

   _____

3. **What's the best compliment you've ever received from someone, and why?**

_____

_____

_____

_____

_____

_____

_____

_____

_____

_____

4. **If you could have any superpower, what would it be, and what would you do with it?**

_____

_____

_____

_____

_____

_____

_____

_____

_____

_____

5. **Who has the biggest influence on you in your life and why?**

_____

_____

_____

_____

_____

_____

_____

_____

6. **What do you think is the key to a meaningful, life-long friendship?**

_____

_____

_____

_____

_____

_____

_____

_____

_____

_____

7. **Do you have an evening or morning ritual? If so, what is it?**

_____

_____

_____

_____

_____

_____

_____

8. **What's your best advice on how to deal with ingratitude, and why?**

_____

_____

_____

_____

_____

_____

_____

_____

_____

_____

9. **How do you motivate yourself when you're feeling depressed?**

_____

_____

_____

_____

_____

_____

_____

_____

_____

_____

10. **What do you value most about friendship? And why?**

_____

_____

_____

_____

_____

_____

_____

_____

_____

_____

11. **What's a flaw you see in yourself currently working on, and why?**

_____

_____

_____

_____

_____

_____

_____

_____

_____

_____

12. **Describe a mistake you made in the past that you've learned from, and do you intend to fix it?**

_____

_____

_____

_____

_____

_____

_____

_____

_____

13. Do you think your life will have drawbacks if you are known for showing ingratitude? If so, what do you see as the drawbacks?

_____

_____

_____

_____

_____

_____

14. Does an attitude of gratitude affect recovery? Circle Yes or No. If yes, how and why?

_____

_____

_____

_____

_____

_____

15. What are you grateful for about your current stage in life?

_____

_____

_____

_____

_____

WORKBOOK G

1. Do you have a friend who gives you sensible productive advice?

   _____

   _____

   _____

   _____

   _____

   _____

2. What's a relationship in your life that gives you lots of feelings of strength and reliability?

   _____

   _____

   _____

   _____

   _____

   _____

3. What is the part of your personality you're grateful for?

   _____

   _____

   _____

   _____

   _____

   _____

4. What is the protection over your life and property that you are grateful for?

_____

_____

_____

_____

_____

_____

5. What is the area of how you were parented for which you feel grateful?

_____

_____

_____

_____

_____

_____

6. Who in your life is always glad to see you? Why?

_____

_____

_____

_____

_____

_____

_____

7. **What pressures are you grateful to have put behind you this year?**

_____

_____

_____

_____

_____

_____

8. **If I asked you what you are grateful for, how many things could you list before you ran out of ideas?**

_____

_____

_____

_____

_____

_____

9. **What is the hardest lesson you were grateful to learn peacefully?**

_____

_____

_____

_____

_____

_____

10. **What aspect of your work or responsibility are you grateful for?**

_____

_____

_____

_____

_____

_____

11. **Has anyone gone out of their way recently to make your life easier or better? How?**

_____

_____

_____

_____

_____

_____

12. **Who is the teacher, supervisor, or mentor whose wise advice you still channel?**

_____

_____

_____

_____

_____

_____

13. **Do you have kids? Circle either "Yes" or "No." If Yes, what are you grateful for about parenting your kids at their current age?**

_____

_____

_____

_____

_____

_____

14. **When was the last time someone was patient with you when you were being a little disturbing and annoying, and you felt grateful?**

_____

_____

_____

_____

_____

15. **Who in your life provides slight, helpful, friendly interactions that brighten your mood whenever you see them?**

_____

_____

_____

_____

_____

_____

16. **What do you see or experience daily that you take for granted?**

_____

_____

_____

_____

_____

_____

17. **What's an item you own that gives you a sense of satisfaction?**

_____

_____

_____

_____

_____

_____

18. **What is the decision you didn't think through but turned out tremendous anyway?**

_____

_____

_____

_____

_____

_____

19. **What is an aspect of your physical wellness you feel grateful for?**

_____

_____

_____

_____

_____

_____

_____

_____

_____

_____

20. **What is something you are looking forward to?**

_____

_____

_____

_____

_____

_____

_____

_____

_____

_____

_____

_____

WORKBOOK H

1. **What are you proud of yourself for?**

   _____
   _____
   _____
   _____
   _____
   _____

2. **What is one positive thing you learn this week?**

   _____
   _____
   _____
   _____
   _____

3. **What gives you aspiration?**

   _____
   _____
   _____
   _____
   _____
   _____

4. **What is one thing you do absolutely well?**

_____

_____

_____

_____

_____

_____

5. **What is one thing that made you laugh recently?**

_____

_____

_____

_____

_____

_____

6. **What is the latest fruit or meal you enjoyed?**

_____

_____

_____

_____

_____

_____

7. **What is the one memory you are grateful for?**

_____

_____

_____

_____

_____

_____

_____

8. **What is one slight achievement you had today?**

_____

_____

_____

_____

_____

_____

_____

9. **Which of your habits are you grateful for?**

_____

_____

_____

_____

_____

_____

10. **What new opportunities have presented itself in your life recently?**

_____

_____

_____

_____

_____

11. **What has brought you satisfaction recently? Why?**

_____

_____

_____

_____

_____

_____

12. **What do you like about yourself, your responsibilities, or your job? Why?**

_____

_____

_____

_____

_____

_____

_____

13. What is a goal you accomplished recently?

_____

_____

_____

_____

_____

_____

_____

_____

14. What awful, dreadful manners have you let go of?

_____

_____

_____

_____

_____

15. How did your emotions help you today? Why?

_____

_____

_____

_____

_____

_____

_____

16. **What are your favorite pets or animals? Why?**

_____

_____

_____

_____

_____

_____

17. **How are you better now than you were a year ago? Why?**

_____

_____

_____

_____

_____

_____

_____

_____

_____

_____

18. **What is your favorite type of music?**

_____

_____

_____

_____

_____

19. **Does your favorite type of music give you a positive and encouraging mood? If yes, please describe your mood then and why?**

_____

_____

_____

_____

_____

_____

_____

_____

_____

20. **Describe your feelings when in a gathering of strangers. Why?**

_____

_____

_____

_____

_____

_____

_____

_____

_____

AUTHOR'S BIO

Patricia Ifeoma Amaram is a veteran of the United States Army, an entrepreneur, writer, and a D.B.A., E.D.D., and P.H.D. scholar. She obtained her M.B.A. in Business Administration with a concentration in Criminal Justice, B.S.C. in Business Administration, and Higher Diploma in Marketing. Before relocating to Atlanta, Georgia, Patricia was also once a Correctional Officer with the Georgia State Corrections Department and a former substitute teacher with Liberty County in Georgia. She is a successful mother of two boys and a servant leader who loves teaching and gardening. Her primary passion is to see the world learn to prioritize kindness, love, and unity in all ramifications.